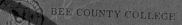

ALCOHOL
The Delightful Poison
a history

ALCOHOL
The Delightful Poison

a history by
ALICE FLEMING

Illustrated with prints and photographs

Delacorte Press/New York

MANUFACTURED IN THE UNITED STATES OF AMERICA

First printing

Designed by MaryJane DiMassi

LIBRARY OF CONGRESS CATALOGING IN PUBLICATION DATA

Fleming, Alice Mulcahey, 1928–
Alcohol—the delightful poison.

1. Drinking customs. 2. Alcoholic beverages.
I. Title.
GT2884.F43 394.1'3 74–22629
ISBN 0–440–01796–3
ISBN 0–440–02524–9 lib. bdg.

GRATEFUL ACKNOWLEDGMENT IS MADE FOR THE USE
OF ILLUSTRATIONS ON THE FOLLOWING PAGES:

4, 48. Trustees of The British Museum

5, 105. The Metropolitan Museum of Art, Museum excavations, 1919–1920; Rogers Fund supplemented by contribution of Edward S. Harkness

7, 10. The Bettmann Archive

16, 20, 22, 25–27, 31, 50, 54, 57–59, 62, 64, 70, 73, 74, 79, 84, 93, 102, 103, 115. The New York Public Library, Picture Collection

25. Hirmer Fotoarchiv, München

35, 74, 83, 90, 91, 94, 95, 118, 128, 129. Wide World Photos

58. The Bostonian Society (Old State House)

87. Underwood & Underwood

130. United Press International

Picture Researcher: Roberta Guerette

Contents

Part I: THE HISTORY OF ALCOHOL

1. The Discovery of Alcohol   3
2. Drinking in History   15
3. Drinking Customs and Ceremonies   24
4. Liquor in the Language   33

Part II: ALCOHOL IN AMERICA

5. From Colonial Breweries to Gin Mills   47
6. The Teetotalers Take Over   61
7. Prohibition: The Noble Experiment   81

Part III: MYTH AND TRUTH

8. The Mystery of Alcoholism   99
9. Myths and Mistakes   111
10. The Sober Truth   121
     Bibliography   133
     Index   135

PART I

THE HISTORY OF ALCOHOL

1

The Discovery of Alcohol

Alcohol has been intriguing and intoxicating human beings for at least seven thousand years. Nobody knows when, how, or by whom it was first discovered, but the chances are good that it happened by accident. When fruit, grain, honey, or any number of other substances are left standing over a period of time, a tiny organism called yeast begins to form in them. The yeast sets in motion a process called fermentation. This in turn produces a bitter-tasting liquid, officially named ethyl alcohol, that can have some startling effects on human behavior.

'Alcohol has turned up in different places at different times and in different forms, but there is scarcely an age or a culture in which it was not known. The Spanish conquistadores found *chicha*, a beer made from fermented corn, among the Indians of South and Central America. The English navigator, Captain James Cook, sampled *kava*, the product of fermented peppers, in the South Sea Islands. The Scottish missionary and explorer, Dr. David Livingstone, penetrated the interior of Africa in 1851 and found the natives enjoying palm wine.

Man's first alcoholic beverage, however, was probably

Egyptian tomb painting depicting wine-bearers bringing various offerings to the master of the tomb, who sits on a very large scale at one end of the scene. The rest of the scene shows the gathering of grapes.

fermented honey or mead. The word *mead* is older than any other word associated with drinking or drunkenness. Etymologists—scholars who study the history of words—have traced it back to several early languages, including Greek and Sanskrit. If the etymologists are correct, mead made from wild honey may have been drunk by the cavemen. It continued to be used in a few parts of the world right up until the 18th century, but in most places mead gradually died out and was replaced by beer or wine.

Man's first alcoholic beverage of which we have any historical record is beer. Clay tablets unearthed from the ruins of ancient Babylon show that the Babylonians were familiar with beer back in 5000 B.C. They considered it a gift from the gods and brewed it in their temples as part of their religious ceremonies. The brewers, all women, were priestesses.

The most avid beer drinkers of the ancient world were the Egyptians. Like the Babylonians, they regarded brewing as a divinely imparted secret, a gift from their goddess of nature, Isis. Every year Egypt's pharaohs consecrated a large quantity of beer in her honor and distributed it to the workers and peasants. The usual allotment was two jugs a day. The rest of the Egyptians bought their beer. For their protection, there was an official superintendent of

Wooden model of bakery and brewery from Tomb of Meket-Re at Thebes; Egyptian Dynasty XI, ca. 2000 B.C.

breweries who made sure that beer sellers offered only the best and purest brews.

Egyptian beer was called *hek*. It was made from barley bread that was crumbled into jars, covered with water, and allowed to ferment. The liquid was then strained off and drunk. For long journeys across the desert, only the fermented bread crumbs were carried. When the travelers reached an oasis, water was added to the jars; the result: instant beer.

At some point in history, brewing was also discovered by the tribes of Northern Europe. There, too, it was involved with religion. The Allemanni, a German tribe, had their beer brewed under the supervision of their priests, who also blessed it before it was consumed. The Vikings not only drank beer in great quantities, they also believed that the spirits of their dead warriors were taken to an enormous banquet hall, Valhalla, where they feasted every night on copious supplies of ale.

The art of brewing probably developed soon after man took up farming. His first crop was grain, from which he made bread. From there it was only a short step to the discovery of fermented grain, from which he made beer. In countries where grapes grew more abundantly than grain, however, the favorite drink was invariably wine.

According to the Bible, wine was discovered by Noah, who planted the first vineyard when he left the ark after the Great Flood. There is also an old Persian legend that credits the discovery to King Jamshid, who ruled Persia several thousand years before the birth of Christ.

Jamshid, so the story goes, was extremely fond of grapes. When one particularly fine harvest produced more than he could possibly consume at his dinner table, he ordered his servants to store the excess fruit in several large jars and put them in the cellars of his palace. Some months later, when the king called for the grapes, he was disappointed to discover that they had burst and the jars

Bible scene, from a woodcut, 1546. The sons of Noah find their father sleeping under a grapevine.

now contained a strange-tasting dark purple juice. Not knowing what to make of this phenomenon, the king sent the jars back to his cellars and instructed his servants to label them POISON.

Not long after that, one of the women of Jamshid's court, feeling lonely and unhappy, decided to commit suicide. She wandered down to the king's cellars, found the jars labeled POISON, and helped herself to a few swallows from one of them. She immediately began to feel better. Then, after a few more swallows, she grew drowsy and fell asleep. When she awoke the next morning, she rushed to tell the king that his "poison" was not poison at all but was actually a pleasant and unusual drink.

King Jamshid promptly sent for some of the "poison" and sampled it himself. He, too, began to feel relaxed and lighthearted. Jamshid thereupon rechristened the mysterious beverage *zeher-e-koosh*, or "the delightful poison," and decreed that thenceforth a share of grapes from every harvest should be preserved in exactly the same manner.

Whether it was discovered by Noah or King Jamshid or by some early vineyard keeper whose name has been lost to history, wine is one of the world's oldest and most widely used drinks. It was known in Mesopotamia as far back as 3000 B.C., it was enjoyed by the Hebrews, the Greeks, and the Romans, and it has, like beer, retained its popularity right into the 20th century.

The wine makers of the present, like those of the past, have produced an almost endless array of wines. Each has a different color, taste, and name depending on the type of grapes that are used, the region it comes from, and the care with which it is made.

The most distinctive of the world's wines, champagne, was invented by a Benedictine monk. In 1668 Dom Pierre Pérignon was put in charge of the wine cellars at St. Peter's Abbey in Hautvilliers in eastern France. Although totally blind in his later years, Dom Pérignon had a highly developed sense of smell and taste, and he was constantly experimenting with new methods of selecting, pressing, and storing his monastery's grapes to produce the best possible wines. One of his experiments led to a pleasant discovery.

Dom Pérignon tried fermenting several types of grapes, then blended them together and let them ferment again. The second fermentation produced an effervescent wine, and when the monk tasted it, he is supposed to have exclaimed, "I am drinking stars."

Dom Pérignon's "stars" were called champagne after the province in which his abbey was located, but although the drink was discovered around 1690, it was over twenty years before it became popular. Many people were suspicious of champagne's sparkle, and it was frequently called the "Devil's wine" or "cork-jumper." It finally came into favor when the duke of Vendôme, looking for a new way to amuse his guests, served it at a gala supper party at his country home near Paris. A troupe of lovely young girls presented each of the guests with a flower-bedecked bottle, and by the end of the evening the champagne had gone to their hearts as well as to their heads.

An interesting sidelight to Dom Pérignon's discovery of champagne was the development of the wine cork. Corks had been used on Roman wine bottles, but they fell into disuse after the decline of Rome. By Dom Pérignon's day the usual wine stopper was a piece of wood wrapped in hemp and dipped in olive oil. After the monk started making champagne he realized that the bubbles would never stay in unless the bottles were more tightly sealed.

Dom Pérignon is supposed to have found a new stopper when a pair of Spanish monks, who were passing through Hautvilliers on a journey north, stopped for the night at St. Peter's Abbey. Their French host, noticing that their

Engraving of sixteenth-century monks making wine in the basement of a monastery. From the painting called "Wine Cellar of the Monastery" by Eduard Grützner; ca. 1890.

water bottles had a strange-looking stopper, asked what it was. The Spaniards explained that it was made from the bark of the cork oak tree, which grew extensively in their country. As soon as Dom Pérignon heard this, he sent to Spain for a batch of the cork bark. It proved to be the ideal bottle stopper for his champagne, and according to the story, corks have been used in wine bottles ever since.

For five thousand years human beings had three intoxicating beverages at their disposal—mead, beer, and wine. All three contained only moderate amounts of alcohol—which simply meant that anyone who wanted to get drunk had to drink more to do it. Somewhere during the 8th century, however, an Arabian named Jabir ibn Hayyan, better known as Geber, devised a process that paved the way for stronger spirits.

Geber was an alchemist, one of an early breed of scientists who flourished during the Middle Ages and dabbled in medicine, magic, and assorted other arts. Like most of the alchemists, Geber was searching for a formula that would transform ordinary metals into gold. One of the numerous experiments he undertook in the search resulted in the discovery of distillation.

Distillation is a chemical process in which a substance is heated until all the impurities are released and only the essential substance remains. Geber burned away the impurities that form in wine during the natural process of fermentation and isolated the essential liquid. It was more concentrated and thus much stronger than the original wine. Geber called it *al kuhul* or "alcohol."

The word *al kuhul* originally referred to a powder Arabian women put on their eyelashes to make them look longer and more lustrous. Scholars suspect that Geber saw a resemblance between the finely ground cosmetic, which was the essence of the metal antimony, and his own discovery, which was the essence of wine.

When Dr. Samuel Johnson compiled his *Dictionary of the English Language* in the 18th century, he noted the connection between unintelligible speech and too much alcohol and concluded that Geber had given his name to the word *gibberish*. Few experts agree with Dr. Johnson, and Geber himself would undoubtedly have been baffled by the suggestion. Although he wrote about his discovery of distillation at great length, he was interested in the process only as a scientific experiment. Neither he nor anyone else saw any practical value in alcohol.

Some five hundred years later, Geber's discovery was dramatically rediscovered by Arnauld de Villeneuve, a 13th-century professor of medicine at the University of Montpellier in France. The alchemists were obsessed with the idea of turning cheaper metals into gold; the physicians were equally obsessed with finding a single cure for every disease. Arnauld de Villeneuve was certain that he had found it in alcohol. He proclaimed it the answer to all man's ills and renamed it aqua vitae, the "water of life." "This name is remarkably suitable," he wrote, "since it is really a water of immortality. It prolongs life, clears away ill-humours, revives the heart and maintains youth."

Other medical men quickly took up de Villeneuve's cry, and before long aqua vitae was being consumed in enormous quantities all over Europe.

Geber's *al kuhul* had been transformed into Arnauld de Villeneuve's aqua vitae. Eventually it became known as brandywine (from the Dutch *brandewijn*, or "burned wine"), and from there it was shortened to brandy. Brandy is still widely used in many parts of the world, but today's drink is a considerably more refined version of the original. It is carefully blended and stored in wooden casks to give it a mellow flavor and a rich golden color.

The most famous type of brandy, cognac, was not developed until the 18th century. It is made from special grapes that grow only in the vicinity of the town of Cognac, France. By law, no brandy can be called cognac unless it comes from there. There are other French brandies, however, and the drink is also made in other countries and from other fruits, such as peaches, cherries, or apples.

A century or two after brandy became the prescribed method for staving off death and disease, Europeans were introduced to still another beverage. It was discovered around 1650 by Francis de le Boe, who was also known as Franciscus Sylvius. Sylvius, a professor of medicine at the University of Leyden in Holland, decided to experiment with distilling the fermented barley that normally produced beer. The result was a liquid that was so unpleasant-tasting that Sylvius disguised its flavor with juniper berries. This new brand of aqua vitae became known as *junever*, the Dutch word for "juniper." When it traveled to France it became *genièvre*, and in England it was shortened to gin. The same drink also found its way to Russia. There they dispensed with the juniper flavoring and called it vodka, or "little water."

Although gin and brandy were the most widely used forms of aqua vitae, they were by no means the only ones. The Scandinavians had their own akvavit, which was made from fermented potatoes and flavored with caraway seeds. The Irish and Scots drank usquebaugh, which means "water of life" in Gaelic. Usquebaugh gave us the English word *whiskey*, which is spelled "whisky" in Scotland and "whiskey" everywhere else. With or without the *e*, whiskey, like gin, is made from grain, but it is distilled in a somewhat different way.

The process begins with barley, which is first malted—covered with water until it begins to germinate—and then cured—heated to dry it out. After that, yeast is added to make it ferment. The result is a liquid much like beer. This is distilled and then left to age in wooden casks for at least three years.

Although the process of making both Scotch and Irish whiskies is the same, there was, and still is, a decided difference in the tastes of the two drinks. The Scots cure their malted barley in peat-burning ovens, which gives their version of usquebaugh a strong smoky flavor.

Scotch whisky is as old or older than gin or brandy, but for centuries its popularity was limited to its native land. Then in 1832 an Irishman, Aeneas Coffey, patented a new type of still that speeded up the process of distillation and enabled whisky to be produced quickly and inexpensively. Coffey's invention was promptly taken over by a group of Scottish businessmen who foresaw great commercial possibilities for their whisky in other parts of the world.

Unfortunately, the Scots had overlooked one major drawback to their plan—few people outside of Scotland

ALCOHOL: The Delightful Poison

could stand its taste. For years their only non-Scottish customers were English distillers who flavored the whisky with juniper and sold it as gin. It was not until almost thirty years after the invention of Aeneas Coffey's still that an Edinburgh distiller, Andrew Usher, hit upon the idea of blending the smoky flavored whisky with a milder ginlike drink that was popular in the Scottish Lowlands. The result was a vastly improved whisky that is now one of Scotland's principal exports.

The Scots consider their whisky the finest in the world, but the Irish are still partial to their own slightly sweeter water of life, and Americans show a strong preference for American-made whiskeys. These come in two varieties— rye, which is made from rye and is produced in both the United States and Canada, and bourbon, an exclusively American drink, which is made from corn and takes its name from the place where it was born—Bourbon County, Kentucky.

Both rye and bourbon were invented at the end of the 18th century. No new types of alcoholic drinks have been discovered since then; but although the date marks the end of the history of alcohol, it is far from the end of alcohol's role in history.

2

Drinking in History

Alcohol is seldom mentioned in history books, but it has affected, and been affected by, many of the events that are. No history of the Jewish people, for example, would be complete without the story of Judith, the beautiful widow who saved the children of Israel from destruction at the hands of an Assyrian army.

On the pretext of bringing an important message to the Assyrian general Holofernes, Judith gained admission to his camp. Captivated by her beauty, Holofernes invited her to have supper with him. In the course of the meal Judith enticed the general into drinking too much wine. When he became drunk and fell asleep, she cut off his head with his own sword.

Judith stole out of the enemy camp, returned to the Israelites, and advised them to attack the Assyrians the next morning at sunrise. When they did, the Assyrian sentries rushed to awaken their general. They entered his tent and discovered his headless body. The word of Holofernes's murder soon spread through the Assyrian camp, and his entire army fled in panic.

Herodotus, a Greek writer who lived in the 5th century B.C., tells of another battle in which alcohol was the

"Judith and Holofernes." From the picture by Horace Vernet.

decisive weapon. Cyaxares, king of Media and Persia, invited his enemies, the Scythians, to a drinking feast. "The greater part of them became intoxicated," Herodotus reported, "and in that state were destroyed. Cyaxares thus obtained possession of Asia."

Wars and invasions have not only been influenced by alcohol, they have, in some cases, led to its wider use. In 218 B.C. the Carthaginian general Hannibal invaded Southern Europe with an army of handpicked troops and began the long march that would take him across the Alps to invade Rome. About halfway along in the march, a group of Hannibal's soldiers grew weary of army life and deserted their general. They settled in the area of Grand Roussillon in southern France, where they planted vineyards and began the production of the wines for which France is now famous. In other parts of France and in Germany and Spain, it was the Roman invaders, the armies of Julius Caesar, who introduced vineyards and taught the natives to appreciate wine.

The Crusades, the long series of wars undertaken by European Christians to wrest the Holy Land from Muslim control, also influenced the making of wine. French Crusaders brought back the Syrah grape from Persia. Syrah grapes are still used in making some of the wines of the Rhone Valley, and they have also been transplanted to Switzerland, Australia, South Africa, and the United States.

In 1190 King Richard the Lionhearted of England organized the Third Crusade. On their way to the Holy Land, Richard and his knights captured Cyprus. The island, just off the coast of Turkey in the Mediterranean Sea, had been famous for its wine for centuries. Richard drank some of it when he and his knights toasted their victory at a banquet.

At the end of the Third Crusade, King Richard gave Cyprus to his knights as a reward for their faithful service. The former Crusaders immediately took over the vineyards and renamed the local wine Commandaria. They built up a thriving business exporting it to England, where it regularly appeared on the royal banquet tables.

The English rule in Cyprus ended in 1489 when the island was annexed by Venice, but less than a century later, in 1571, it was captured by the Turkish sultan Selim II. A notorious wine lover, Selim was nicknamed "the Sot." It is quite possible that he conquered Cyprus just to assure himself of a lifetime supply of its wine.

Commandaria is still produced on Cyprus. A sweet wine made from a blend of both red and white grapes, it has the distinction of being the oldest wine to be known by a specific name.

The battle of Culloden in 1746 not only influenced the course of English history but also gave the world a new drink. In 1745 Prince Charles Edward Stuart organized an army of Scottish Highlanders and led an expedition against England. The Stuarts had been deposed from the English throne by the Glorious Revolution of 1688, and Bonnie Prince Charlie was determined to regain it. Instead, his army was defeated by the duke of Cumberland at Culloden Moor, and the young prince was forced to flee for his life. He hid out in the Scottish Highlands until a Scotswoman, Flora MacDonald, smuggled him onto the Isle of Skye. From there, the MacKinnon family helped him escape to France.

As a reward for their assistance, the grateful prince gave the MacKinnons the secret formula for his personal liqueur, a sweet, strong brandy flavored with Scotch whisky. The MacKinnons kept Bonnie Prince Charlie's formula to themselves for 160 years, but in 1906 they decided to market it commercially. Originally *an dram budheach*, which in Gaelic means "the drink that satisfies," its name was later corrupted to Drambuie. Today it is one of the most popular after dinner drinks in the world.

In the past and sometimes in the present as well, important political decisions have been made over a lifted glass. The Saxons, who ruled England in the 7th and 8th centuries, never sat down to their councils until they had each had a ration of beer. They drank it out of a large stone mug passed around from hand to hand. In ancient Greece dinner parties were usually followed by a symposium, or "drinking together." In both Sparta and Athens these developed into drinking clubs, and the men who belonged to them became a powerful political force.

In the past, good rulers recognized the importance of beer and wine in their subjects' lives and in their country's economy. The emperor Charlemagne, who ruled Western Europe at the beginning of the 9th century, personally supervised the planting of vineyards and the brewing of beer in his kingdom. The Domesday Book, a survey of England compiled by order of William the Conqueror, included extensive information about the making of wine and the cultivation of grapes. The Magna Charta, which deprived England's kings of their absolute power, also contained a clause regulating the measurement of the nation's ale and wine.

At least one English ruler owed his downfall to alcohol. In 946 Edward the Elder was invited to a feast at a church in Gloucestershire. He and his companions got drunk and were unable to defend themselves when they were attacked and murdered by a band of their political enemies.

During the Middle Ages wine was as valuable as money. Some feudal lords actually paid their debts with it. Needless to say, grape growing and wine making became serious businesses. There were strict laws against stealing grapes and against making inferior wines and trying to pass them off as better ones. In many places wine counterfeiters were executed. Grape thieves got off easier. They were forced to march through the village with their hands locked above their heads in a wooden vise. There was a bell attached to the vise that rang as they trudged through the streets and summoned the villagers to come out and jeer at them.

One ruler, Philip the Bold, duke of Burgundy, was not above making laws to regulate grapes as well as grape thieves. In 1395 he banned the Gamay grape from Burgundy's vineyards because it gave the wine a "very great and horrible harshness."

Europe's vineyards were originally planted and tended by farmers. With the spread of Christianity, however, wine making was gradually taken over by the various religious

Engraving of medieval farm scene showing the gathering of grapes for wine-making.

orders. Because wine was used in the Christian Mass and in the sacrament of Holy Communion, the monks regarded its production as part of their religious duties. After the fall of Rome in the 5th century A.D., the monks were among the few people in Europe who knew the technique of making fine wine.

One of the many religious men who took an interest in the production of wine was St. Martin, who became bishop of Tours in A.D. 371. Martin spent much of his time visiting the vineyards of the Loire Valley and talking to the monks about their work. According to an old legend, St. Martin once visited a monastery in Anjou and tied his donkey to a post beside a grapevine. The bishop spent several hours inspecting the monks' vineyards and cellars. When he was ready to leave, he discovered that his donkey had been nibbling on the grape leaves and had devoured them right down to the trunk of the vines. The bishop apologized for his four-footed companion, but the following year the monks noticed that the shoots that had been destroyed grew back more abundantly and produced fatter, more luscious grapes. Learning a lesson from St. Martin's donkey, the monks of Anjou began pruning their vines on a regular basis and saw a remarkable improvement in the flavor of their wines.

The religious orders in France were stripped of their lands after the French Revolution, but many of the drinks they developed are still in existence. Chablis, one of the best-known white wines, was originally made by the Cistercian monks at their abbey in Chablis. The formula for the liqueur chartreuse was developed in 1605 by the monks of the Carthusian order, after whom it was named. Another popular liqueur was born at the Benedictine monastery in Fécamp when one of the monks added a mixture of herbs and plants to ordinary brandy. King Francis I of France passed through Fécamp in 1534, tasted the

Engraving of an eighteenth-century sugarcane plantation in the West Indies, showing the cutting of sugarcane.

new drink, Benedictine, and soon made it famous all over Europe.

In 1770 Captain James Cook claimed the continent of Australia for Great Britain. The colony later became a dumping ground for criminals and political undesirables, but Australia's original settlers had expected to turn it into England's vineyard. When the first colonists sailed for Australia in 1788, they brought with them a collection of vines. They were the first to be planted in the new country, and until Australia's monetary system was established, the wine they produced served as the colony's currency.

Explorers introduced, and were introduced to, new drinks in the lands they visited. One drink that was brought back to Spain by Christopher Columbus's crew was rum. It was made from fermented molasses obtained from the sugarcane that grew so abundantly in the West Indies. English explorers to the New World also sampled the drink, and it became even more popular in England than it was in Spain. For years every sailor in the British

Navy was issued a daily ration of rum, and in the days when Britannia ruled the waves, it was often said that rum was the real power of the British fleet.

Still further evidence of alcohol's place in history can be found in the story of the Pilgrims' arrival in America in the winter of 1620. The passengers on the tiny ship *Mayflower* had intended to explore the New England coast more thoroughly before selecting a place to settle, but they cut their voyage short and landed at Plymouth Rock. In his *History of Plimouth Plantation*, their leader, William Bradford, explained why: "For we could not take much time for further search and consideration, our victuals being much spent, especially beer."

Whether the founding of one of America's first colonies can be attributed solely to a short supply of beer is open to question. Few historians would deny, however, that intoxicating drinks have played a lively role in our country's history ever since.

3

Drinking Customs and Ceremonies

Alcohol has always been involved with a great many customs and ceremonies. Wine is used at the Jewish Seder and the Christian Communion service, champagne is used for christening ships, and there are few countries where drinkers don't offer a toast or touch glasses before taking their first sip.

Many of the rituals involving alcohol began as expressions of the awe and respect human beings felt for this mysterious beverage.

In both Babylon and Egypt, beer was regarded as a gift from the gods. The Babylonians and Egyptians regularly offered beer to the goddess of fertility in the hope that she would bless their crops. The Egyptians also left jugs of beer in their tombs for the spirits of the dead to enjoy.

In Greece and Rome, wine was the favorite drink, and there, too, it was believed to have supernatural origins. The Greek god of wine, Dionysus, supposedly invented the art of wine making in his youth. When he grew to manhood, he wandered about the world teaching men how to cultivate vineyards and make wine. The Greeks had many festivals in honor of Dionysus; wine was drunk in abun-

Dionysus at sea with miraculous vine; Greek, 535 B.C. Detail.

Drawing of "Orgy and Bacchanal" from the painting by Bernard Picart. In Rome, the term bacchanal applied to the feasts in honor of Ceres as well as to those in honor of Bacchus. In both, wild, disheveled dancing was the custom.

Woodcut shows Dionysus sitting on a bull, holding a grape branch and pouring wine from the pitcher.

dance at all of them. The ceremonies also included sacrificing a goat to the god. The goat may have been chosen to die because goats often nibbled on the shoots in vineyards and ruined the grapes. The feasts of Dionysus were always associated with music, singing, and dancing. Greek drama developed out of the celebrations, and Dionysus also came to be honored as the god of the theater.

Dionysus's counterpart in both Greek and Roman mythology was Bacchus. He was depicted with a crown of grapes on his head and a wine goblet in his hand. In Rome the festivals honoring Bacchus were called Bac-

Engraving depicting the Feast of Passover. Engraving by Oppenheim from a painting by A. Harland.

chanalias. They were originally solemn religious observances but eventually turned into such drunken orgies that in 186 B.C. the Roman Senate banned them.

According to Hebrew tradition, wine drinking began with Noah, who made the first wine from the vineyard he planted when he emerged from the ark. Wine has always occupied an important place in Jewish life. It is mentioned in the Bible no less than 165 times, and most of the references are favorable. Every week on the night before the Sabbath, devout Jews give thanks to God at the evening meal, and the head of each family offers special prayers over bread and wine.

The feast of the Passover, the most important in the Jewish calendar, is marked by an initial meal called the Seder, in which wine is served as part of the religious observance. The Christian sacrament of the Eucharist, or the Lord's Supper, as it is called in some faiths, is a direct outgrowth of the Passover ceremony.

Jesus and his apostles were celebrating the Passover at the Last Supper when Jesus blessed the bread and wine, gave it to his apostles, and told them to continue making the same offering in his memory. Bread and wine are now used in Christian religious services as an offering to God in commemoration of Jesus's crucifixion. In most denominations real wine is used, but a few temperance-minded congregations substitute unfermented grape juice.

In addition to its use in worshiping God, alcohol has also been closely involved in men's relationships with each other. During the Middle Ages, religious orders offered bread and wine to travelers who appeared at the doors of their monasteries. In England the monks gave their guests bread and beer. The tradition is continued today at the Hospital of St. Cross in Winchester.

Bishop Henry de Blois, who founded the Hospital in 1140, instituted the Winchester or Wayfarers' Dole. He ordered the Hospital staff to give bread and ale to anyone who asked for it. The modern Winchester Dole is offered only to a limited number of visitors and is given mainly to keep the old custom from dying out.

During the 17th and 18th centuries the English expression for any type of celebration was "cakes and ale." Before that, social gatherings were usually known simply as "ales." Many of them were organized under the auspices of the church, and they usually included dancing, games of bowls, and food as well as drink.

There were all kinds of ales. The church ale was given by the churchwardens who made beer and sold it at the festival to raise money for the parish. At Easter time there was a clerk ale at which the money raised from selling beer was presented to the parish clerk. The Whitsun ale celebrated the coming of the Holy Spirit on Whitsunday, or Pentecost, seven weeks after Easter. Help ales were given for the benefit of a church member who had fallen ill or suffered some similar misfortune. Give ales honored deceased parishioners who left a bequest to the church to pay for an ale at which they would be remembered. The bride's ale celebrated a wedding. The bride always poured the ale at the feast, and the custom has given us the word *bridal*.

For the English, ale was not only a festive drink; it was also the most appropriate way to solemnize a wide variety of occasions. Tenant farmers paid their landlords in tithes —a tenth part of their crop—and received a tithe ale as their receipt. When an apprentice entered a new trade, it was customary for him to present his master with a foot ale, so called because the young man was getting his footing in the trade.

Another old English custom, the wassail bowl, is remembered today in a few of our Christmas carols. The word *wassail* comes from the Saxons, who, when they drank with a friend, saluted his health with the words "*Wes hal,*" meaning "Be hale." For many years a wassail bowl—

29

a large bowl of spiced ale—was carried from door to door in every English parish on New Year's Eve. The parishioners were invited to drink from it and in return gave an offering to the church for the new year.

Still another old English drinking custom is the loving cup. Today a loving cup is a large double-handled silver cup presented to the winner of a contest. In times gone by, a cup of this type was passed around at banquets, and the guests all drank from it. In Scotland it was called a grace cup. It was supposedly introduced by St. Margaret, a 10th-century Scottish queen, to entice the Scots into remaining at the dinner table long enough to say grace after the meal.

When the loving cup or grace cup was passed, it was customary for each person to drink from it and for the person next to him to stand while he did so. This ritual started after the Danish invasion of England in the 10th century. The English were not allowed to drink in the presence of their Danish conquerors without permission. If an Englishman did take a drink, he could expect to be slain on the spot for his disobedience. The English soon became wary of drinking in front of the Danes, even when they had permission, so whenever a Dane invited an Englishman to drink with him, the Dane always stood at his side to pledge his safety while he drank.

"Good health," "Cheers," and similar expressions of goodwill before drinking are called toasts. They received the name because at one time it was customary to put a piece of toasted bread into beer or wine to improve its flavor. After the loving cup was passed around at a banquet, it was returned to the host, who drank the last of it, then ate the piece of toast in honor of his guests. Eventually the toast was no longer added to the drink, but the verbal toast remained.

It is not uncommon for drinkers to clink their glasses when they offer a toast. This practice dates back to the

Dark Ages when people were baffled by drunkenness. The best explanation they could find for it was that the Devil entered a person's body when he opened his mouth to drink. Clinking glasses supposedly frightened him away. For the same reason, some primitive tribes used to ring a bell before drinking, and in Bulgaria it was customary to make the sign of the cross.

Today it is considered good manners for a host to take a sip of wine before serving it to his guests. This is to be sure that it has not gone sour and that there are no bits of cork floating on the top. The practice originated many centuries ago and for somewhat different reasons. During the Middle Ages it was not uncommon to kill an enemy by slipping poison into his wine. The host who took the first sip assured his guests that he had no intention of poisoning

Medieval drawing showing a servant tasting the wine before serving in order to detect poison meant for the guests.

them and thus invited them to relax and enjoy themselves.

Taking the first sip of wine was also a custom in the days before corks, when hemp dipped in oil was the usual bottle stopper. Often some of the oil was left on top of the wine, and the thoughtful host took the first sip so none of his guests would be forced to drink it.

Modern restaurants sometimes adhere to another old custom—having the sommelier, the waiter in charge of the wine, wear a shallow silver cup suspended from a chain around his neck. The chain symbolizes the fact that the sommelier, like the wine stewards of medieval times, holds the keys to the wine cellar. The cup, called a *tastevin*, is for sampling the wine to make sure it is of good quality.

Champagne is often served on festive occasions and is also widely used for christening ships. The rituals of ship launching started with an old pagan rite. In the earliest days of seafaring, sailors felt a need for special protection against the storms and ill winds they so often encountered on the high seas. Whenever they built a new ship they offered elaborate prayers to the gods before it was put into use. The ship and her crew wore flowers, an altar was erected on deck, and a priest poured wine and oil over the vessel and placed it under the protection of a goddess, whose statue was carved on the prow.

The Vikings prayed for the safety of their vessels by offering human sacrifices to the gods. They slid their ships into the water over the bodies of the victims and then sprinkled their blood on the bows. Red wine, commemorating the blood, was originally used in christening ships, but it was later replaced by champagne.

Alcohol is one of man's oldest discoveries, so it is hardly surprising that so many traditions have developed around it. What is surprising is that so many of them have persisted until the present day—proof perhaps that even 20th-century drinkers are still in awe of "the delightful poison."

4

Liquor in the Language

One of the most noticeable effects of alcohol is on the tongue. After one or two drinks, people become more relaxed and talkative. If they drink more, they start to slur their words and lose track of what they are saying. If they keep on drinking, their speech becomes garbled and incoherent. Drinking also has an effect on the tongue in another sense. It has contributed an unusually large number of words and phrases to the English language.

The expression "drunk as a lord," for instance, goes back to medieval times when wine was so expensive that only the nobles could afford to drink great quantities of it. "Mind your p's and q's," meaning be careful of your behavior, grew out of a system that was used in the English public houses, or pubs. Ale was served in either pint or quart tankards, and the pubkeeper kept a slate on which he marked how many p's and q's each customer drank. The pubkeeper who minded his p's and q's never lost money; the customer who did the same avoided getting drunk.

The expression "Dutch courage," false courage inspired by drinking, originated in the 17th century, when there was a great deal of bad feeling between the English and the Dutch. The English cast a slur on the Hollanders' drinking habits as well as their bravery when they invented the phrase to describe someone who becomes more daring under the influence of alcohol.

The tumbler or drinking glass may have gotten its name from the curved horns in which the Saxons put their beer. The beer had to be drunk in one gulp because the horns wouldn't stand upright. Eventually someone thought of adding a weight to the bottom of the horn so beer could be drunk at a more leisurely rate. The containers no longer tumbled over, but they continued to be called tumblers just the same.

The word *bootlegger*, meaning anyone who sells liquor illegally, was widely used during Prohibition when illegal liquor was the only kind there was. The term *bootleg* existed long before the adoption of the Eighteenth Amendment, however. It dates back to the days when the government first started imposing taxes on whiskey. Distillers were required to purchase tax stamps and display them on their whiskey barrels. Determined to avoid the tax, some distillers affixed the stamps to the barrels, then removed them after delivery and used them again on the next shipment of whiskey. Since the tax stamps were concealed in the deliverymen's boots, the illicit whiskey became known as bootleg whiskey.

A few distillers and many more private whiskey makers avoided government taxes by making their whiskey in secret. They set up stills in out-of-the-way locations and as a further precaution usually worked at night with the moon providing their only light. The practice of making illicit whiskey soon became known as moonshining, and the whiskey was called moonshine. Moonshining is still common in Tennessee, Kentucky, and other parts of the rural South. Since whiskey of this type is not aged, it has the clear color and raw taste of pure alcohol, making its other name, "white lightning," most appropriate.

In the early days of whiskey making, whiskey was

Illegal stills of the 1930's.

shipped to liquor dealers in large wooden barrels instead of in bottles. Each distiller burned or branded his name on the head of his barrels. (The opposite end, called the government head, was used for federal tax stamps.) The distiller's name soon came to be called the brand name, a term that now refers to the name a manufacturer gives his product.

Almost every big city has a rundown section where alcoholics congregate. Usually it's known as Skid Row. The original Skid Row was in Seattle, Washington. The city's first sawmill was built in 1852 in the Pioneer Square district, near Puget Sound. The logs were dragged into the mill over a set of tracks or skids, and the area became known as Skid Road. As Seattle grew and developed, Pioneer Square fell upon hard times, and Skid Road (which somehow got shortened to Skid Row) became what the term means today, a hangout for drunks and vagrants.

There are many versions of how the word *cocktail* came into being. According to one story, doctors used to swab the throats of their patients with a mixture containing alcohol. The instrument they used was a long curved feather taken from a rooster's tail. Patients supposedly liked the treatment so much that they began asking for one of the "cock's tails" even when their throats weren't sore.

Another story traces the invention of the cocktail to the American Revolution and gives the credit to a barmaid named Betsy Flanagan who worked at a tavern in Elmsford, New York. The tavern, a popular meeting place for American colonists, happened to be right near a farm owned by a loyalist. One day Betsy Flanagan vowed that she would steal some of the Tory's chickens and treat her fellow patriots to a chicken dinner.

When she did, she celebrated the occasion by decorating the bar with tail feathers. That night a slightly drunk patron came in and demanded a glass of the "cock's tails." Betsy poured in a couple of different ingredients, mixed them together, stuck a feather in the glass, and if the story is true, served the nation's first cocktail.

It is also possible, however, that the word *cocktail* has nothing to do with roosters' feathers. During the 18th century "cocktail" was the name for a carriage horse whose tail was clipped short and stood upright like a cock's tail. Since these horses were never thoroughbreds but a mixture of several breeds, it is possible that the mixed drink called a cocktail might have been given their name.

Equally possible is the story that the cocktail was a Mexican invention. An Aztec nobleman supposedly created an intoxicating drink from the sap of the cactus plant and was so proud of it that he sent his daughter Zochitl to present it to the emperor. Pleased with both the drink and its bearer, the emperor married Zochitl and named the drink in her honor. American soldiers were introduced to the Zochitl (which sounded to their ears like "cocktail") during the Mexican War, and began inventing their own cocktails after they returned home.

Nobody has ever tried to explain how the highball, a tall drink of whiskey mixed with soda or water, got its name. It may have come from railroad terminology. The highball is a signal, given by raising the arm, meaning the track is clear, full speed ahead. By raising his glass, the drinker may be indicating that he is ready to go full speed ahead on a drinking spree.

Alcoholic beverages are often referred to by other names. Some people drink "hooch," others prefer "the sauce," still others like a "drop" or a "nip." One of the most common expressions for alcohol is "booze." The word supposedly commemorates E. C. Booze, a 19th-century distiller who made a whiskey called Old Log Cabin. Old Log Cabin never became popular, but booze is known all over the country.

Of the thousands of slang expressions in the English language, by far the greatest number are concerned with drinking or getting drunk. Benjamin Franklin once compiled a list of the ones that were used in his day. He published it in the *Pennsylvania Gazette* in 1733 under the title "The Drinker's Dictionary."

THE DRINKER'S DICTIONARY

A.

He is Addled.
He's casting up his Ac-
    counts.
    Afflicted.
    in his Airs.

B.

He's Biggy.
    Bewitched.
    Block and Block.
    Boozy.
    Bowz'd.
    Been at Barbadoes.
    Drunk as a Wheel-
        barrow.
    Burdock'd.
    Busky.
    Buzzey.
Has stole a Manchet out of
    the Brewer's Basket.
His head is full of Bees.
Has been in the Bibbing
    Plot.
        drank more than he
        has Bled.
He's Bungey.
        As drunk as a Beggar.
He sees the Bears.
He's kiss'd Black Betty.
        had a thump over the
        head with Samp-
        son's Jawbone.
        Bridgey.

C.

He's Cat.
    Cagrin'd.
    Capabe.
    Cramp'd.
He's Cherubimical.
    Cherry Merry.
    Wamble Crop'd.
    Crack'd.
    Concern'd.
    Half way to Concord.
Has taken a Chirriping-
        Glass.
    Got Corns in his head.
    A Cup too much.
    Coguy.
    Copey.
He's beat his Copper.
    Crocus.
    Catch'd.
He cuts his Capers.
He's been in the Cellar.
    In his Cups.
    Non Compos.
    Cock'd.
    Curv'd.
    Cut.
    Chipper.
    Chickery.
    Loaded his Cart.
    Been too free with the
        Creature.
Sir Richard has taken off his
        Considering Cap.
He's Chap-fallen.

D.

He's Disguiz'd.
    Got a Dish.
    Killed his Dog.
    Took his Drops.
It's a Dark Day with him.
He's a Dead Man.
Has Dipp'd his Bill.
He's Dagg'd.
    seen the Devil.

E.

He's Prince Eugene.
    Enter'd.
    Wet both Eyes.
    Cock Ey'd.
    Got the Pole Evil.
    Got a brass Eye.
    Made an Example.
    Eat a Load & a half
        for breakfast.
    In his Element.

F.

He's Fishey.
    Fox'd.
    Fuddled.
    Sore Footed.
    Frozen.
    Well in For't.
    Owes no man a Far-
        thing.
    Fears no Man.

    Crump Footed.
    Been to France.
    Flush'd.
    Froze his Mouth.
    Fetter'd.
    Been to a Funeral.
His Flag is out.
He's Fan'd.
    Spoke with his Friend.
    Been at an Indian
        Feast.

G.

He's Glad.
He's Grostable.
    Gold-headed.
    Glaiz'd.
    Generous.
    Booz'd the Gage.
    As Dizzy as a Goose.
    Been before George.
    Got the Gout.
    Had a Kick in the
        Guts.
    Been with Sir John
        Goa.
    Been at Geneva.
    Globular.
    Got the Glanders.

H.

He's Half and Half.
    Hardy.
    Top Heavy.

Got by the Head.
Hiddey.
Got on his little Hat.
Hammerish.
Loose in the Hilts.
Knows not the way
    Home.
Got the Hornson.
Haunted with Evil
    Spirits.
Has taken Hippocrates'
    Grand Elixir.

I.–J.

He's Intoxicated.
Jolly.
Jagg'd.
Jambl'd.
Going to Jerusalem.
Jocular.
Been to Jerico.
Juicy.

K.

He's a King.
Clips the King's Eng-
    lish.
Seen the French King.
The King is his
    Cousin.
Got Kib'd Heels.
Knapt.
Het his Kettle.

L.

He's in Liquor.
Lordly.
He makes Indentures
    with his Leggs.
Well to Live.
Light.
Lappy.
Limber.

M.

He sees two Moons.
Merry.
Middling.
Moon-eyed.
Muddled.
Seen a Flock of
    Moons.
Maudlin.
Mountous.
Muddy.
Rais'd his Monuments.
Mellow.

N.

He's Eat the Cocoa Nut.
Nimptopsical.
Got the Night Mare.

O.

He's Oil'd.
Eat Opium.

Smelt of an Onion.
Oxycrocium.
He's Overset.

P.

He drank till he gave up his
    Half Penny.
Pidgeon Ey'd.
Pungey.
Priddy.
As good condition as a
    Puppy.
Has Scalt his Head Pan.
Been among the
    Philistines.
In his Prosperity.
He's been among the
    Phillippians.
contending with
    Pharaoh.
Wasted his Paunch.
Polite.
Eat a Pudding Bag.

Q.

He's Quarrelsome.

R.

He's Rocky.
Raddled.
Rich.
Religious.

Lost his Rudder.
Ragged.
Rais'd.
Been too free with Sir
Richard.
Like a Rat in Trouble.

S.

He's Stitch'd.
Seafaring.
In the Sudds.
Strong.
Been in the Sun.
He's as Drunk as David's
    Sow.
Swampt.
His Skin is full.
He's Steady.
He's Stiff.
He's burnt his Shoulder.
He's got his Top Gallant
    Sails out.
Seen the yellow Star.
As Stiff as a Ringbolt.
Half Seas over.
His Shoe pinches him.
Staggerish.
It is Star-light
    with him.
He carries too much
    Sail.
Stew'd.
Stubb'd.
Soak'd.

Soft.
Been too free with Sir John Strawberry.
He's right before the wind with all his Studding Sails out.
Has sold his Senses.

T.

He's Top'd.
Tongue-ty'd.
Tann'd.
Tipium Grove.
Double Tongu'd.
Topsy-Turvey.
Tipsey.
He's swallowed a Tavern Token.
He's Thaw'd.

He's in a Trance.
He's Trammel'd.

V.

He makes Virginia Fence.
Valiant.
Got the Indian Vapours.

W.

The Malt is above the Water.
He's Wise.
He's Wet.
He's been to the Salt Water.
He's Water Soaked.
He's very Weary.
Out of the Way.

Some of the expressions listed in "The Drinker's Dictionary," such as "stew'd" and "oil'd," are still used. Most of them, however, have been replaced by new words coined by new generations of drinkers. Some appeared in the 19th century when the Irish immigrants talked about "having a bun on" or "getting soused." More came during Prohibition when expressions like "fried," "to have a snootful," "plastered," and "pickled" were born.

The origin of some of the synonyms for drunkenness is a mystery, but it is not hard to see where others, such as "pie-eyed," "tangle-footed," "sloppy," "fuzzy," and "zigzag," came from. Another highly descriptive term that was used in New England in the mid-19th century is "howcome-ye-so." It isn't hard to imagine a wife asking her husband the question when he came reeling home from the local tavern.

An unusually large number of the words for drunkenness are nautical expressions, which may prove the theory that sailors have a special fondness for drinking. A few expressions, like "three sheets to the wind" and "under the weather," are still used; others, like "decks awash" and "half seas over," are obsolete.

One of the most interesting facts about the various synonyms for drunkenness is that they tend to divide into three categories reflecting three different stages of inebriation. A person who has taken one or two drinks is said to be "feeling good," "rosy," "mellow," or "merry." If he keeps on drinking, he will get "woozy," "weak-jointed," or "higher than a kite," and if he doesn't have enough sense to stop, he will wind up "rigid," "paralyzed," "stone blind," "knocked for a loop," or "under the table."

Benjamin Franklin once commented on the lengths to which people will go to avoid using the word *drunk*. "It argues some Shame in the Drunkards themselves," he wrote, "in that they have invented numberless Words and Phrases to cover their folly."

This is undoubtedly true, but it is also true that people hesitate to talk openly about things they do not understand, and drunkenness has been, and still is, one of those things.

PART II

ALCOHOL IN AMERICA

5

From Colonial Breweries to Gin Mills

The English have been drinkers since the days of the Anglo-Saxons, so it is hardly surprising that the English-born founders of America's first colonies counted beer among the necessities of life.

In 1607, thirteen years before the Pilgrims reached the shores of Massachusetts, another band of Englishmen established a settlement at Jamestown, Virginia. Two years later, the governor of the new colony advertised in England for two brewers to be dispatched to Virginia as quickly as possible.

In New England most of the settlers included brewers in their company. One of the first crops they planted was barley, from which they hoped to make beer. When the barley did not thrive, they turned to apple trees and made fermented cider or applejack instead.

The Dutch who settled New Amsterdam also liked strong drink. In 1640 their governor, Willem Kieft, set up America's first distillery on Staten Island. Later Kieft also built the first tavern on Manhattan Island. When the English took over the colony in 1664 and New Amsterdam became New York, the distillery stopped making the Dutch favorites, brandywine and gin, and took to making

' *Pictorial map showing "The Arrival of the Englishmen in Virginia," taken from a copy of "A briefe and true report of the new found land of Virginia" by Thomas Harriot; printed at Frankfurt in 1590.*

rum, which by then had become the most popular drink in America.

The manufacture of rum began in New England sometime around 1650. The colonists in Massachusetts and Rhode Island had originally hoped to become farmers, but it did not take them long to realize that New England's thin soil and harsh climate made farming on a large scale impossible. They turned to fishing and lumbering and began trading their products in the West Indies for the islands' chief export, molasses. The New Englanders used the molasses for making rum, and before long, the shrewd Yankee traders had worked out a clever and profitable method for disposing of their rum. The history books call it the Triangular Trade.

The points of the triangle were a New England port, such as Boston or Newport, Rhode Island, the Gold Coast of Africa, and a port in the West Indies, usually Kingston, Jamaica. New England sailing ships carried the rum to Africa, where it was traded for slaves. The slaves were taken to the West Indies and traded for molasses. The ships then sailed home, where molasses was made into rum and the whole trading process began all over again.

The rum trade made New England merchants rich, contributed to the design of faster sailing ships, and earned Yankee captains a reputation for fine seamanship. Unfortunately, however, the West Indians sold most of their slaves to plantation owners in America's South, which meant that the Triangular Trade was directly responsible for the growth of slavery in the United States. In the 19th century wealthy New Englanders were among the staunchest supporters of the abolitionist movement to free the slaves. At least some of their dedication may have been inspired by guilty consciences over the way their ancestors had amassed their fortunes.

Most of the New England rum trade was with the French-, Dutch-, and Spanish-owned islands of the West Indies. This angered the English, who also had territory there and wanted the colonists to trade only with them. In 1733 Parliament passed the Molasses Act, which imposed a tax on every gallon of foreign-made molasses that was imported into America.

As one of the first of a long list of British laws regulating colonial taxes and trade, the Molasses Act is sometimes listed among the causes of the American Revolution. As a matter of actual fact, however, the colonists' only reaction to the law was to ignore it. Far from being considered a crime, smuggling became an act of patriotism, and New England's sea captains became artists at sneaking their cargoes past British customs inspectors. In a single year, 1763, some fifteen thousand hogsheads of molasses were imported into Massachusetts, but taxes were paid on only a thousand.

When James Oglethorpe founded the colony of Georgia in 1733, he gave each settler forty-four gallons of beer and expressed the hope that they would never drink anything stronger. Unfortunately, Oglethorpe also made the mistake of giving each of his colonists sixty-five gallons of molasses, which they promptly used for making rum.

By the end of their first year of colonization almost all of Georgia's settlers had been stricken with some type of disease. Oglethorpe blamed their illnesses on "the excessive drinking of rum punch," and at his behest Parliament passed a law banning rum and brandy in the colony of Georgia.

Instead of improving the colonists' drinking habits, however, the new law only made them worse. They slowed

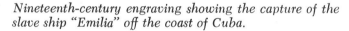

Nineteenth-century engraving showing the capture of the slave ship "Emilia" off the coast of Cuba.

down their efforts to build up the colony and spent most of their time figuring out ways to get their hands on something to drink. Stills were set up in the woods, barrels of rum were smuggled in by ship from South Carolina, and drunkenness became more of a problem than illness had ever been.

It soon became apparent that Georgia's prohibition law did not work. People caught breaking it simply demanded a trial by jury, and since even Georgia's most respectable citizens saw nothing wrong with drinking bootleg liquor, the juries rarely found anyone guilty. The prohibition law was finally rescinded in 1742, and Georgia's colonists stopped worrying about rum and turned their attention to more important matters.

Rum was the most widely consumed drink in the American colonies right up until the Revolution. A colonial poet writing about the inhabitants of Derry, New Hampshire, observed:

> It was often said, that their only care,
> And their only wish, and only prayer,
> For the present world, and the world to come,
> Was a string of eels and a jug of rum.

When twenty-six-year-old George Washington was trying to get elected to the Virginia House of Burgesses in 1758, he distributed seventy-five gallons of rum to the voters of his district and won the election without difficulty. Before setting out on his famous midnight ride in 1775, Paul Revere is said to have stopped at the home of Isaac Hall in Medford. Hall, a captain in the minutemen and a rum distiller by trade, gave Revere two drafts of rum to fortify him for his journey.

Drinking played a prominent role in the American Revolution. In the tense days before the dispute between England and her colonies finally erupted into war, committees of correspondence and the Sons of Liberty often held their meetings in taverns. It seems safe to assume that many of the discussions took place over a tankard of rum. In Boston the headquarters for the disgruntled colonists was the Green Dragon Inn on Union Street. It was there that the Boston Tea Party was organized. Sam Adams and John Hancock frequently met at the Black Horse in Winchester, and Captain John Parker, commander of the minutemen at Lexington, established his headquarters at Buckman's Tavern on the Lexington green.

In 1808 Congress passed a law forbidding the further importation of slaves. This brought the Triangular Trade to an abrupt halt, but the popularity of rum was already on the wane. Americans were rapidly discovering a new drink, whose ingredients could be produced on their own soil—whiskey.

The earliest American whiskey was rye, which was made from rye grown by farmers in Maryland, Pennsylvania, and Virginia. George Washington raised rye at Mount Vernon and converted it into whiskey in his own still. A second type of American whiskey developed soon after the Revolution when bands of Scotch-Irish immigrants began trekking along the Wilderness Road into Kentucky. One of the first crops planted by the new settlers was corn, and one of the first things they made from it was whiskey.

The original batch of Kentucky whiskey is said to have been made in 1789 by the Reverend Elijah Craig, a Baptist minister who lived just outside of Georgetown in what was then Bourbon County. The whiskey was named after the county, and the county had been named after King Louis XVI of France—whose family name was Bourbon—in gratitude for his support of America in her war for independence.

America's first whiskey distillers were farmers who

made only enough for their own consumption. As more and more settlers moved into Kentucky and western Pennsylvania, however, whiskey became essential to their economy. There were no decent roads in or out of the new regions, and goods had to be shipped to eastern markets by packhorse. A horse that could carry only about four bushels of corn or rye could carry six times that amount if the grain was converted into liquid form. With an eye to selling as much of their crop as possible, the western farmers quickly took up whiskey making. Rye and bourbon became as valuable as money and were commonly used in its place.

Two years after George Washington was sworn in as first president of the United States, the backcountry distillers suffered a major blow to their economy. Congress, at the urging of Secretary of the Treasury Alexander Hamilton, voted to levy a tax on whiskey. The move brought screams of outrage from the farmers. Many of them refused to pay the tax and were hauled into court. There were a number of public protests against the tax, and finally, in 1794, rioting broke out in western Pennsylvania. A federal marshal in Allegheny County was attacked for trying to enforce the hated law, and an angry mob set fire to the home of the regional tax inspector and threatened to march on Pittsburgh.

The Whiskey Rebellion was the first test of whether the new government of the United States was going to enforce its laws or submit to mob rule. President Washington acted swiftly and decisively. He first sent a delegation to western Pennsylvania to try to reason with the rebellious farmers. When their efforts failed, he dispatched an army of militiamen to keep order in the area and authorized the immediate arrest of anyone who persisted in defying the government. The Whiskey Rebellion collapsed almost at once, and although the Pennsylvania farmers remained

In the West, tar and feathers entered politics again in 1794. In this engraving a group of Whiskey Rebels escorts a federal tax collector from his burning home.

lasting foes of both George Washington and Alexander Hamilton, they knuckled under and obeyed the law.

The American president whose name is most often associated with whiskey is Ulysses S. Grant. When Grant was commander of the Union Army during the Civil War, there were repeated rumors that he drank too much. On more than one occasion visitors to the White House advised President Abraham Lincoln to remove Grant for his intemperance. Lincoln, who was more interested in Grant's abilities as a general than in his personal habits, ignored them. His reply to one such adviser was, "If I knew what brand of whiskey he drinks I would send a barrel or so to some other generals."

Grant had been a heavy drinker as a young man when he was separated from his wife and assigned to an army post in Oregon. In later years, however, he usually abstained from alcohol, and many historians now believe that the stories about his drinking habits were, for the most part, untrue. Nevertheless, Grant seemed to be haunted by whiskey.

In 1876, during his second administration as president, Treasury Department investigators uncovered a conspiracy among a group of St. Louis whiskey distillers to defraud the government of almost three million dollars in whiskey taxes. There was further evidence that part of the money had gone to finance Grant's campaign for a second term and that his private secretary and close friend, Orville E. Babcock, was involved in the conspiracy. The Whiskey Ring was a major scandal of Grant's administration, and although the President was personally innocent of any wrongdoing, it did little to enhance his reputation as a statesman.

Another politician, James G. Blaine, was done in by alcohol before he even got to the White House. Blaine ran on the Republican ticket against the Democrat, Grover Cleveland, in 1884. The campaign was a vicious one and was further complicated by the fact that a large body of Republicans refused to support Blaine, and the leader of Tammany Hall, the Irish-dominated Democratic organization in New York, detested Cleveland.

Tammany's votes looked like the key to a Blaine victory until a Presbyterian clergyman, the Reverend Dr. Samuel Burchard, speaking at a dinner for Blaine, denounced the Democratic party as the party of "Rum, Romanism, and Rebellion." After this attack on both their religion and their drinking habits, New York's Irish Catholics voted solidly against Blaine and helped to ensure Grover Cleveland's election to the presidency.

At various times, both rum and whiskey were numbered

among America's most popular beverages, but beer, the favorite of the early settlers, by no means disappeared. When William Penn built Pennsbury Manor, his splendid home in Bucks County, Pennsylvania, he insisted on having a brewhouse on the property. George Washington ordered daily rations of beer issued to his troops, and during the bitter winter of 1777–78 when his ragged army was encamped at Valley Forge, he regularly wrote to the Continental Congress, begging them to send him more guns, food, and beer.

Thomas Jefferson made beer at his Virginia estate, Monticello, and his fellow Virginian, James Madison, was so eager to encourage American brewing that in 1789, during his term in Congress, he introduced a bill levying a tax on foreign-made beers.

The first wave of German immigrants began coming to the United States in the 1840's. They brought with them a taste for beer as well as their own recipes for making it. German immigrants established breweries in such cities as New York, Milwaukee, and St. Louis and made both brewing and beer drinking an important part of American life.

Although somewhat indirectly, beer also played a role in the fight for women's rights. In 1861 a Poughkeepsie, New York, brewer named Matthew Vassar set aside part of his sizable fortune to establish Vassar College, one of the country's earliest colleges for women and the first women's school to be supported by a large endowment.

Inns and taverns had been the center of social and community life in the United States since colonial times. After the immigration of thousands of Irish during the Potato Famine of 1848, the inns and taverns in the cities where the Irish clustered gradually gave way to saloons. Out of place in a strange land, rejected by native-born Americans, and forced to live in poverty and squalor, many of the newcomers found their only consolation in

Nineteenth-century painting showing the original Schaefer Brewery, Nineteenth Street and Broadway, New York, 1842.

Drawing by H. R. Blaney (1894) showing the famous Green Dragon Tavern on Union Street in Boston.

Nineteenth-century drawing showing New Yorkers enjoying a mug of beer at a local tavern.

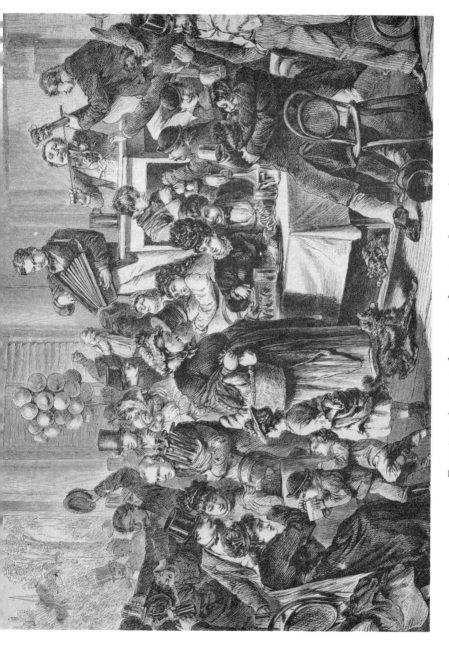

Drawing of a typical nineteenth-century beer garden.

alcohol and spent most of their time in these neighborhood "gin mills."

Drunkenness was by no means a new problem in American life, but it was a problem that was becoming increasingly difficult to cope with. The country had changed from a nation of small farms and shops to a nation of factories, where absenteeism and poor performance seriously interfered with production. In addition, drunkenness was starting to create social problems. Many drunkards wound up in jail or in public almshouses. Others deserted their jobs and families and became vagrants, living in the streets and begging money to buy cheap whiskey or beer.

During the 19th century, a movement to prohibit the manufacture and sale of alcoholic beverages began in the United States. The question sharply divided the country and provided the story of alcohol in America with its longest and liveliest chapters.

6

The Teetotalers
Take Over

In the early days of the United States, most people thought that human beings could not exist without alcohol. Men and women, old and young, rich and poor, regularly started the day with a morning dram. The drink might be anything from cherry brandy to wine mixed with sugar and water, as long as it contained alcohol. A daily glass of "bitters" was considered essential for warding off disease, clearing the head, and keeping the heart in good working order.

The morning dram was often only the beginning of the day's drinking. Community activities—repairing the public road, helping with a barn raising, or bringing in the harvest—always called for plenty of drinks all around.

Businessmen and shopkeepers kept barrels of rum on tap for favorite customers. Since it was an accepted fact that no man could do a hard day's work without the aid of alcohol, laborers were given a break for bitters at 11:00 A.M. The bitters was usually rum, supplied at their employer's expense, but in the hat factories in Danbury, Connecticut, it was an apple brandy called "gumption." Farmers, equally solicitous of their hired hands, placed

61

Benjamin Rush, late eighteenth-century prohibitionist. Engraving by J. B. Longacre from a painting by Sully.

jugs of rum behind the bushes and let the men help themselves as they toiled in the fields.

This free and easy attitude toward alcohol was responsible for a great deal of drunkenness among Americans of all ages and social classes. Nevertheless, the idea persisted that alcohol was one of life's necessities. The first person to suggest that it was not was Dr. Benjamin Rush.

Rush, a signer of the Declaration of Independence and a surgeon in the Continental Army, was one of the country's first and most prominent physicians. In 1784 he published a treatise entitled *An Inquiry into the Effects of Spiritous Liquors on the Human Mind and Body*. The treatise condemned the use of "ardent spirits," arguing that they caused, among other things, obstruction of the liver, jaundice, hoarseness, diabetes, epilepsy, gout, madness, and "frequent and disgusting belchings."

Like those of most doctors of his era, Rush's medical opinions were not very scientific. He believed, for instance, that alcohol ruined the texture of the hair, and he advised people to protect themselves from chills and fever in bad weather by pouring rum into their boots. Still, Rush was a highly respected physician, and many Americans, particularly those who were already alarmed by the growing problem of drunkenness, took his warnings against alcohol quite seriously.

One of the first results of Benjamin Rush's treatise was that a group of Connecticut businessmen decided to stop serving rum to their employees and give them only cider or beer. A second result was that it prompted a New York physician, Dr. Billy J. Clark, to do something about the drunkenness in his own community. Clark enlisted the aid of the pastor of the First Congregational Church of Moreau, in Saratoga County, and together the men organized the first temperance society in the United States. The Union Temperance Society was founded in 1808; it pledged its forty-four members to "use no rum, gin, whisky, wine or any distilled spirits . . . except by the advice of a physician, or in case of actual disease, also excepting wine at public dinners."

The pledge, which left considerable leeway for a drink now and then, wrought no great reforms in Saratoga County, but the Society did become a model for a number of similar organizations in other parts of the country. It also proved an important point. When the members of the Society got together after upholding their pledge for a full year, they discovered to their surprise that they had not only suffered no ill effects from not drinking, but had also been able to work more efficiently.

The early temperance societies took a fairly lenient approach to alcohol. Like Benjamin Rush, they were against "ardent spirits"—rum, whiskey, and brandy—but they had no objections to weaker drinks like cider, wine, and beer. Moreover, although they condemned drunkenness, they argued for moderation in drinking, rather than total abstinence.

Alcohol found a more dedicated and vociferous foe in the Reverend Lyman Beecher, a Presbyterian minister and

The Mawney House, in which the first temperance society
was organized. Original organizers included the Rev. L.
Armstrong, Dr. B. J. Clark, Gardiner Stow and James
Mott (pictured above).

father of Harriet Beecher Stowe, the author of *Uncle Tom's Cabin*. The Reverend Mr. Beecher, inspired by Dr. Benjamin Rush's treatise against alcohol, began preaching against strong drink as early as 1810. He became even more outspoken on the subject after his appointment as pastor of a church in Litchfield, Connecticut. Reverend Beecher urged his congregation to join him in a crusade to save the country from "rum-selling, tippling folk, infidels and ruff-scruff." He led the way by organizing the Connecticut Society for the Reformation of Morals, which was dedicated to suppressing not only drinking but gambling as well.

In many parts of the country, opposition to alcohol was closely tied to a dislike of Thomas Jefferson and his Anti-Federalist party. The Federalists, led by Alexander Hamilton, had been instrumental in putting through the tax that led to the Whiskey Rebellion in 1794. The Anti-Federalists, who had opposed the tax, were popularly regarded as friends of whiskey. Thus, anyone who disliked Thomas Jefferson or his party was likely to be found in the ranks of the temperance movement. Not surprisingly, when a group of Massachusetts clergymen tried to form their own version of the Connecticut Society, they received strong support from Federalist politicians.

Within a decade after Lyman Beecher began denouncing alcohol, the war against drinking had grown into a national conflict. Beecher preached against it almost constantly. His sermons were printed and distributed throughout the country, and thousands responded by rallying to the temperance cause. Before long, America's drinking habits began to show signs of change. Employers stopped serving drinks to their workers; farmers no longer left a jug of rum in the fields. Liquor rations were discontinued in the United States Army, and the sale or use of liquor was prohibited at military bases.

These changes only made Lyman Beecher eager for

further reforms. In 1826 he and a group of Bostonians founded the American Society for the Promotion of Temperance, later called the American Temperance Union. The Union, led mainly by Protestant clergymen, set up state and local chapters and urged its members to sign a pledge promising to abstain from intoxicating liquors. The Union also had a second, more ambitious goal—to persuade the legislatures of every state to pass laws against the production and sale of alcohol.

When it was first organized, the American Temperance Union opposed whiskey, rum, and brandy but saw no harm in beer, wine, and cider. A few of its members, however, frowned on alcoholic beverages of every kind. At the annual meeting of the Union in 1836, the conservatives joined forces and pushed through a proposal pledging all its members to "total abstinence from all that can intoxicate."

Before long, the temperance advocates had earned the nickname "teetotalers." The word originated in England and is said to have been coined when a man who stuttered stood up at a British temperance meeting and called for a pledge of total abstinence. "We can't keep 'em sober unless we have the pledge total," he insisted. "Yes, Mr. Chairman, tee-tee-total."

Before the teetotalers took over, there were some five thousand branches of the American Temperance Union in the United States and over one million people had signed the pledge. With the adoption of the new stricter pledge, membership in the Union began to decline. Many onetime supporters were convinced that total abstinence was an unnecessary as well as an unreasonable goal.

The American Temperance Union lost much of its impact, but the temperance cause was by no means dead. In 1840 another organization, the Washington Temperance Society, burst on the scene with a more dramatic approach to the problem of drunkenness. The Society was organized by six men who used to meet regularly at Chase's Tavern in Baltimore and spend their evenings getting drunk. One night two members of the sixsome, out of curiosity, attended a temperance lecture by a New York clergyman, the Reverend Matthew Hale Smith. Smith's eloquence had an almost miraculous effect on the two men. They not only came away resolved to give up alcohol, but returned to Chase's Tavern and persuaded their former drinking companions to do the same.

The men immediately organized the Washington Temperance Society and within six months had enrolled almost a thousand members. The Washingtonians, as they were called, were all reformed drunkards and could thus lecture with authority on the evils of alcohol. Their technique was simple. They described their own experiences as drunkards in vivid detail, then asked other drinkers in the audience to step forward and sign the pledge.

One of the Washingtonians' most gifted lecturers was John H. W. Hawkins, a Baltimore hatter who had given up drinking after fifteen years. Hawkins traveled around the country and made over five thousand speeches on behalf of temperance. He specialized in heartrending stories; his favorite was the tale of how he had been inspired to reform after his daughter Hannah came to him with tears in her eyes and begged, "Papa, please don't send me for whiskey today!"

Although the Washingtonians were the most effective organization to appear thus far, they were never able to win support from the older temperance societies. For one thing, they had no interest in working for Prohibition laws. For another, they never mentioned God, sin, or the Devil in their lectures. What annoyed the other temperance advocates most about the Washingtonians, however, was that they allowed tavernkeepers to join their Society. They did not care how much liquor a man sold to other people as long as he pledged not to drink himself. In the long run, however, it was not lack of support from other reformers that caused the Washingtonian movement to die out. Their appeal was highly emotional, and emotion is impossible to sustain over a long period of time.

As the Washingtonians were dying out, still another temperance movement was coming to the fore. On July 1, 1849, an Irish priest, Father Theobald Mathew, arrived in the United States. Three years before, Father Mathew had organized the Catholic Total Abstinence Society in the slums of Cork. The movement spread through Ireland and inspired some half million drunkards to reform.

Although most American Protestants disliked both Catholics and Irishmen, Father Mathew was given a warm welcome by the United States government and was guest of honor at a banquet given by President Zachary Taylor. Drunkenness was a major problem among the country's Irish immigrants, and Father Mathew's Catholic Total Abstinence Society looked like a good way to solve it. The priest did have phenomenal, although not always lasting, success. Between his arrival in the United States in the summer of 1849 and his departure a little more than two years later, he traveled some thirty-seven thousand miles and administered the pledge to half a million Catholics.

Although Father Mathew set up an American branch of his Catholic Total Abstinence Society, the temperance movement in the United States was, for the most part, dominated by Protestants. Their zeal was inspired to a great extent by prejudice. Drinking was a favorite diversion of the Catholic immigrants who lived in the big cities. Native-born Americans, predominantly Protestant farmers, had no use for these poor, illiterate, and often unruly intruders. They hoped to both punish and reform them by closing down their saloons.

America's teetotalers spread their message in many ways. Several organizations published their own magazines and pamphlets. Individual members wrote novels and short stories in which alcohol was always the villain. There were songs, too. One, "The Saloon Must Go," declared:

I stand for prohibition
The utter demolition
Of all this curse of misery and woe;
Complete extermination
Entire annihilation
The Saloon must go.

Many temperance advocates regarded the stage as only slightly less disreputable than the saloon. Others, recognizing the fact that preaching reached more people when it was disguised as entertainment, took to writing plays. Two of the most popular temperance dramas were *The Drunkard or The Fallen Saved* and *Ten Nights in a Bar-Room and What I Saw There*. The latter featured a song, "Come Home, Father," sung by a little girl. It begins, "Father, dear Father, come home with me now, the clock in the belfry strikes one . . ." and continues through the hours until the baby brother dies and it is too late for the father to be of any help even if he should come home.

Ten Nights in a Bar-Room was adapted from a story written by T. S. Arthur in 1854. It recounts the experiences of a traveler who visits the town of Cedarville at various times over a ten-year period. In the course of each visit, something dreadful occurs at the local saloon. First the little girl who comes to fetch her father home is killed by a glass thrown during a drunken brawl. Later in the play, the saloonkeeper's wife goes insane and his son murders him. Finally the citizens of Cedarville band together, close down the saloon, and outlaw alcohol forever. The play ends with all of them looking forward to a new and happier life.

TEN NIGHTS IN A BAR-ROOM.
A TEMPERANCE DRAMA, IN FIVE ACTS.
BY WILLIAM W. PRATT.
First Performed at the National Theatre, New York, September, 1858.

𝔇𝔯𝔞𝔪𝔞𝔱𝔦𝔰 𝔓𝔢𝔯𝔰𝔬𝔫𝔞𝔢.

[*See page 6.*

SAMPLE SWICHEL ...	Mr. Yankee Locke.
SIMON SLADE	Mr. A. W. Young.
JOE MORGAN	Mr. A. Fitzgerald.
FRANK SLADE	Mr. G. Edeson.
HARVEY GREEN	Mr. J. M. Ward.
MR. ROMAINE	Mr. J. Nunan.
JUDGE HAMMOND...	Mr. E. W. Thompson.
WILLIE HAMMOND	Mr. R. S. Meldrum.
NED HARGRAVE	Mr. Porter.
JUDGE LYMAN	Mr. H. F. Stone.
TOM PETERS	Mr. Cheesbrough.
MRS. SLADE...	Miss Colbourne.
MRS. MORGAN	Mrs. J. J. Prior.
MRS. HAMMOND	Mrs. Bradshaw.
MARY MORGAN	Miss Plunkett.
MEHITABLE CARTRIGHT...	Miss Rosa Cline.

TIME OF REPRESENTATION.—One Hour and Forty Minutes.

No. 944. Dicks' Standard Plays.

A playbill advertising "Ten Nights in a Bar-Room."

A law against alcohol was passed by popular acclaim in *Ten Nights in a Bar-Room*. In real life, it was more difficult. The temperance advocates' goal, a complete ban on alcohol, became easier to achieve after the United States Supreme Court ruled in 1833 that state governments could regulate the liquor trade within their own borders. The ruling also permitted local option, which meant that individual counties and towns were free to adopt Prohibition laws if they wished.

At the state level, Massachusetts was the first to act. A law passed in 1838 prohibited the sale of spirits in anything less than fifteen-gallon lots. The law was aimed directly at lower-class drinkers who could not afford to buy that much whiskey at one time. They evaded it, however, by buying fifteen gallons and a gill. They then drank the gill, returned the fifteen gallons, and got their money back. It soon became obvious that the Fifteen Gallon Law was impossible to enforce, and the legislature quickly repealed it.

The next state to take up the fight was Maine. There, the leading temperance spokesman was Neal Dow, a tannery owner and banker who was also mayor of Portland. In 1851, after almost two decades of argument and agitation, Dow persuaded Maine's legislature to pass the nation's first statewide Prohibition law. It was a major victory, and teetotalers all over the country were ecstatic. "The glorious Maine law," declared Lyman Beecher from his pulpit, "was a square and grand blow right between the horns of the Devil."

Neal Dow's feat inspired temperance advocates in other states to redouble their efforts. They organized marches, staged demonstrations, and sent petitions to their legislators. In response to their demands, thirteen states followed Maine's example and passed Prohibition laws.

The Civil War brought the temperance movement to a temporary halt. Many teetotalers were also abolitionists, and they turned their full attention to working for the freedom of the slaves. Their main accomplishment during the war was to get the rum ration for sailors abolished in the United States Navy. In addition, they never lost an opportunity to blame alcohol when a general who was known to drink lost a battle.

After the war, the teetotalers pursued their own war against drinking with renewed vigor. By now most of the temperance organizations were working for Prohibition. In 1869 one group organized the Prohibition party, which ran its own candidates for state offices and in 1872 nominated James Black, a Pennsylvania lawyer, to run for president. Black condemned the manufacture and sale of alcoholic beverages as "high crimes against society" and promised to work for the passage of a constitutional amendment that would give the United States universal and permanent Prohibition.

Needless to say, Black did not win the election. Later Prohibition party candidates, including the redoubtable Neal Dow, were equally unsuccessful. The party is still in existence, but even in its best year, 1892, it never polled more than 271,000 votes.

During the 19th century, women were denied the right to vote, but they still managed to make themselves heard on the subject of Prohibition. Women's Crusades sprang up in New York, Ohio, Illinois, and Michigan. Their usual tactic was to march into a tavern or grogshop, read an appeal to the owner asking him to close down his business, and conclude their visit by singing a hymn and reciting the Lord's Prayer. Sometimes a "praying band" of women gathered on their knees outside a saloon, and occasionally the crusaders just stood silently at the saloon door, writing down the name of every man who stepped inside.

In addition to the women's groups, Sunday school children were also recruited in the fight for temperance. One band of youngsters, the Cold Water Army, had its own uniforms and an official pledge:

Drawing showing "Women Crusaders," a temperance group, pleading with a saloon keeper to close his saloon.

Photograph of Mrs. Rutherford B. Hayes (Lucy Ware Webb Hayes) who served nonalcoholic drinks at the White House, earning her the name "Lemonade Lucy."

Photograph of Carry Nation, temperance leader. Undated.

We do not think we'll ever drink,
Whiskey or gin, brandy or rum,
Or anything that'll make drunk come.

In 1874 the Women's Crusade developed into a national organization, the Women's Christian Temperance Union. One of its leaders, Frances E. Willard, also campaigned for woman suffrage. Another prominent member of the WCTU was Mrs. Rutherford B. Hayes, wife of the nineteenth president of the United States. "Lemonade Lucy," as she was called, vowed to uphold her beliefs by serving no alcohol in the White House during her husband's administration.

A White House steward found a way to circumvent the First Lady's decision. He concocted a delicacy called Roman Punch, which was made with egg whites, sugar,

74

lemon juice and, unbeknownst to Mrs. Hayes, laced with a hearty dash of rum. This treat was served at the sherbet course midway through every state dinner and was known among White House regulars as the Life Saving Station.

The adoption of the Maine law in 1851 had been an important milestone for the teetotalers. A second victory came in 1880 when Kansas wrote a Prohibition law into her state constitution. But there were setbacks, too. Of the thirteen states that had already passed Prohibition laws, nine had either repealed them or had declared them unconstitutional. Elsewhere, Prohibition laws were introduced in a number of state legislatures and were voted down. Soon only Maine, Kansas, and North Dakota remained dry. Even there bootleggers and "blind pigs"— illicit taverns—did a thriving business. The temperance societies, after more than a half century of effort, were still a long way from ridding the nation of alcohol.

The year 1893 marked a significant turning point. The Reverend Howard Hyde Russell organized the Anti-Saloon League at the First Congregational Church of Oberlin, Ohio. The League mounted a well-planned drive that eventually led to the adoption of the Eighteenth Amendment to the United States Constitution and gave the country Prohibition.

Political action was not a new idea in the temperance movement, but the Anti-Saloon League took a different approach to politics. Instead of supporting one particular party, they threw their weight behind individual candidates regardless of party. Moreover, their support was not limited to men who actively campaigned for Prohibition. The League's policy was not to worry too much about the present but to support candidates who would be likely to vote for Prohibition in the future.

While the Anti-Saloon League worked quietly behind the scenes, other reformers preferred to be in the limelight. The most famous was Carry Nation, who in 1899 launched a one-woman crusade against alcohol which she called her "hatchetation." She barged into an illegal saloon in Kiowa, Kansas, and demolished the bar with a hatchet. Later she did the same thing to other saloons not only in her home state but elsewhere around the country.

On the strength of the publicity she received for her saloon wrecking, the fifty-three-year-old teetotaler went on the road lecturing against alcohol and selling souvenir hatchets to her audiences. Carry Nation received enthusiastic support from some quarters. Her "hatchetation" was endorsed by the WCTU and by many Protestant clergymen. In most places, however, she was treated as a joke. After pictures of her saloon-smashing sprees appeared in the newspapers, several liquor manufacturers wrote her letters of thanks for advertising their products. Some saloons served Carry Nation cocktails and decorated their bars with hatchets and signs saying, "All Nations Welcome but Carry."

Carry Nation eventually died in a mental hospital, and it seems more than likely that she was emotionally disturbed for much of her life. The Anti-Saloon League wisely ignored her. While Carry Nation dominated the headlines, the League went on quietly working toward its announced goal—national Prohibition. By 1900 they had succeeded in getting a number of towns and counties to adopt dry laws under local option. They were now ready to tackle state legislatures.

Their first conquest was Georgia in 1907. Oklahoma came next, and within six years some half dozen other states had fallen into line. The Anti-Saloon Leaguers were encouraged not only by the number of states adopting Prohibition laws but by the fact that so many of them were in the South, long known as one of the hardest-drinking areas of the country. Whether they were aware of it or not, the South's change of heart was motivated largely by the fact that in the postslavery era, outlawing liquor helped keep the blacks under control.

Despite the growing number of local laws against alcohol, the Prohibitionists had forgotten one thing. There were no laws against mail order sales of liquor in dry areas. Several thriving businesses had already been founded for the purpose of selling whiskey by mail to drinkers stranded in Prohibition states. The drys were determined to close them down. They succeeded when Congress passed the Webb-Kenyon Law in 1913. The law, a significant triumph for the drys, gave each state the right to make its own laws about such shipments.

The year 1913 also marked the twentieth anniversary of the founding of the Anti-Saloon League. At its annual convention that year, the members voted to start working toward their final goal—an Eighteenth Amendment to the United States Constitution that would provide for nation-wide Prohibition. The drive was kicked off by a march on Washington, with the marchers singing their theme song, the all too prophetic "A Saloonless Nation in 1920."

The Anti-Saloon League began its efforts with the congressional election of 1914. They set up headquarters in Protestant churches around the country and began working to elect their candidates. As a result of the League's efforts in 1914, a substantial number of Prohibition-minded candidates were sent to Congress. One of them, Representative Richmond P. Hobson of Alabama, introduced a resolution calling for the Eighteenth Amendment. Hobson's resolution was defeated by a narrow margin, but the Anti-Saloon League simply waited two years until the next congressional election, increased their strength in Congress, and vowed to try again.

The Sixty-fifth Congress, which convened in March, 1917, had as one of its first orders of business the declaration of war against Germany. After this, laws were needed to put the country on a wartime basis. One was a measure to control the production and distribution of food. The drys, who helped draw up the bill, had a clause inserted outlawing the manufacture and sale of alcoholic beverages because of the need to conserve grain.

The opponents of Prohibition—the wets, as they now called themselves—were not very happy about the possibility of a wartime ban on alcohol. In an attempt to get the drys to abandon the measure, they agreed to let the Senate vote on a resolution introduced by Senator Morris Sheppard of Texas calling for a prohibition amendment to the Constitution.

The resolution would have to be passed by both the Senate and the House of Representatives and then be ratified by majorities in two-thirds of the state legislatures. The process would take a long time, and the wets were convinced that the amendment would be defeated anyway. To make sure it was, Senator Warren G. Harding of Ohio persuaded the drys to accept an addition to the resolution stating that the amendment had to be ratified within seven years. This addition was supposed to be the final guarantee that the Eighteenth Amendment would fade into oblivion.

To the dismay and astonishment of the wets, however, it did not work. The Eighteenth Amendment whizzed through Congress and was ratified by thirty-six state legislatures in a little over a year. On January 16, 1919, the amendment was officially adopted; national Prohibition would go into effect a year later. Eventually all but two states ratified the Eighteenth Amendment. Rhode Island and Connecticut were the lone holdouts.

The credit for the adoption of Prohibition belongs primarily to the Anti-Saloon League, which by now had supporters in every state legislature in the country. To a certain extent, however, the move toward Prohibition was spurred on by the emotional climate created by World War I. People felt that they ought to be making sacrifices

Cartoon inspired by the Volstead Act of 1919 by Rollin Kirby, called "Prohibition." In a sarcastic comment on a detested law, this lantern-jawed rapscallion is leading his disciples in a chorus of "My Country 'Tis of Thee."

for the war effort and alcohol seemed like a logical thing to give up. Patriotic sentiment was further exploited by rumors that the country's brewers, who were mostly of German descent, were plotting to demoralize Americans by selling them beer.

Ironically, the wartime Prohibition law that the wets had expected to be forgotten in the furor over the Eighteenth Amendment was not forgotten at all. A bill forbidding the use of grain for making whiskey was passed in both houses of Congress in 1917. Later beer and wine were included in the ban, and the sale of all intoxicating drinks was forbidden after July 1, 1919. The war was over by the time this part of the law went into effect, but the restrictions on manufacturing liquor created severe shortages and gave the public a foretaste of what Prohibition would be like.

Before the Eighteenth Amendment could go into effect, a law had to be enacted to spell out how it was going to be enforced. In October, 1919, Representative Andrew J. Volstead of Minnesota introduced the National Prohibition Act, better known as the Volstead Act. The law provided for the padlocking of hotels and restaurants that sold intoxicating liquors (which were defined as anything containing more than 0.5 percent alcohol) and allowed for a search of such premises and a seizure of any illegal alcohol found there. Private individuals who had bought liquor prior to the passage of the Volstead Act were allowed to keep it, and brewers could continue manufacturing beer as long as they reduced its alcoholic content to the required 0.5 percent.

The Volstead Act passed both the House of Representatives and the Senate in record time, and on January 17, 1920, a year after the adoption of the Eighteenth Amendment, a new era—the Age of Prohibition—began.

7

Prohibition: The Noble Experiment

The teetotalers had high hopes for the United States under the Eighteenth Amendment. One member of the WCTU called Prohibition "God's present" to the country; and an Anti-Saloon Leaguer predicted, "A new nation will be born."

In Norfolk, Virginia, the flamboyant evangelist Billy Sunday held a funeral service for John Barleycorn with the Devil as chief mourner. "The reign of tears is over," Sunday declared in his funeral oration. "The slums will soon be only a memory. We will turn our prisons into factories and our jails into storehouses and corncribs. Men will walk upright now, women will smile, and the children will laugh."

Not everyone accepted Billy Sunday's rosy view of the future, but few Americans doubted that John Barleycorn had indeed been laid to rest. Drinkers who could afford to had started buying up wines and whiskey as soon as the Eighteenth Amendment was ratified. As the date of its enforcement drew near, the rush to lay in supplies of liquor grew more and more frantic. Trucks, cars, and even baby carriages were pressed into service transporting bottles from liquor stores and distilleries before they shut down.

Some of the country's hotels and restaurants served the last of their liquor at Prohibition Eve parties, but the atmosphere was generally more doleful than festive. Drinkers saw no reason to celebrate, and the hotel and restaurant owners were in an equally gloomy mood. Within the next few years many of them would be forced to close their doors for lack of customers.

In Washington government officials had worked out what they thought was a foolproof system to enforce the Volstead Act. A Prohibition Bureau was set up as a division of the Treasury Department. John F. Kramer, a former temperance leader from Ohio, was appointed Prohibition Commissioner, and a force of fifteen hundred federal agents was hired to apprehend violators.

"This law," Kramer declared optimistically, "will be obeyed in cities, large and small, and in villages, and where it is not obeyed it will be enforced. . . . The law says that liquor to be used as a beverage must not be manufactured. We shall see that it is not manufactured. Nor sold, nor given away, nor hauled in anything on the surface of the earth or under the earth or in the air."

The Prohibition Commissioner and his staff expected to have no problems enforcing the law. A Treasury official in New York confidently predicted, "There will not be any violations to speak of."

Less than twenty-four hours after Prohibition went into effect, federal agents seized one liquor shipment in Peoria, Illinois, and another in New York City, raided stills in Detroit and Hammond, Indiana, and issued warrants for the arrest of twelve other violators of the Volstead Act.

It soon became obvious that the law designed to make Americans stop drinking was having precisely the opposite effect. The people who were determined to drink, drank.

Photo shows the captured power boat "Baboon" at Phila-delphia on December 22, 1931, as Coast Guard sailors began removing contraband liquor, estimated to be worth $50,000. The vessel was seized by the Coast Guard in Delaware Bay.

By a curious twist of fate they also seemed to drink more often and in larger quantities. New York, which had boasted fifteen thousand bars before Prohibition, now had an estimated thirty-two thousand speakeasies—undercover drinking spots where customers often had to whisper a password before they could be admitted.

Another completely unexpected effect of Prohibition was that women and young people, who up until the 1920's had never been a large force in the nation's drinking population, suddenly decided it was the smart thing to do.

In addition, a new invention, the hip flask that could be tucked into purses as well as pockets, made drinks available at any hour of the day or night.

Near beer, the weak 0.5 percent alcohol mixture that was legally available, appealed to very few drinkers. Most people wanted stronger stuff, and they usually got it. There were several sources of supply. One was liquor manufactured outside the United States and smuggled into the country. Some was brought across the border from Canada or Mexico by car or truck. More came in by ship from Europe, Cuba, and the West Indies.

The rumrunners, as the ships were called, were converted yachts, fishing trawlers, tramp steamers, any kind of vessel that could be pressed into service. They anchored along the Atlantic and Gulf coasts at a point known as

Prohibition cartoon "Four Out of Five Have It" by John Held, Jr., the famous cartoonist of the 1920's.

Rum Row—just outside the three-mile limit that marked the end of U.S. territorial waters.

In the beginning, anyone was welcome to come out and buy, and they came in everything from canoes to outboard motorboats. Later, the three-mile limit was extended to twelve miles, and larger, faster boats were needed to haul in the cargo. Rumrunning soon became a job for professionals. Best known of these was the man who claimed to have founded Rum Row, Captain Bill McCoy.

McCoy's second claim to fame was the invention of the burlock, a pyramid-shaped package of six whiskey bottles encased in straw and sewn up in a burlap bag. The burlock gave the bottles as much protection as a wooden crate but took up less space and was easier to carry.

Bill McCoy always took great pride in the high quality of the liquor he sold. He boasted that it was "the real McCoy"—a phrase that McCoy, along with a half dozen other McCoys, insisted he had invented.

Most of the liquor that was smuggled into the United States was the real McCoy. The liquor that was made here illegally usually wasn't. Some—the least harmful—was diluted with water to make it go further. But there were also more dangerous mixtures. Industrial alcohol, used in making perfumes, insecticides, paints, and the like, was still legal, and many bootleggers set up phony chemical plants so they could buy it. Unfortunately, not all industrial alcohol was pure. Much of it was methyl or wood alcohol, a deadly poison; the rest was often denatured—mixed with methyl alcohol to make it unfit to drink.

Bootleggers who didn't know any better—or worse, didn't care—were apt to wind up poisoning their clients, who often went blind or became fatally ill, as did many people who tried making their own whiskey out of hair tonic, rubbing alcohol, or automobile antifreeze. During one three-day period in 1928, twenty-five New Yorkers died from drinking denatured alcohol.

In the South, Jamaica ginger was frequently used in making bootleg whiskey. It had a high alcoholic content, but it also caused a disease popularly called jakitis that resulted in paralysis of the legs and feet. It has been estimated that at least fifteen thousand Americans were crippled by jakitis during the years the Eighteenth Amendment was in effect.

Most bootleg liquor was made and sold by gangsters, but in a few places, ordinary and otherwise law-abiding citizens set up businesses of their own. Backwoods farmers who had been running illegal stills for years suddenly discovered that there was money in "moonshine." Italian immigrants who always made their own wine anyway, started making more of it and selling it for a profit.

Americans who wanted to save money or preferred not to deal with bootleggers took to drinking "home brew" or "bathtub gin." Since it was physically impossible as well as unconstitutional for Prohibition agents to search every home in America, the Volstead Act was in effect unenforceable. There was no way the government could prevent people from manufacturing intoxicating beverages in their own kitchens, bathrooms, or cellars.

As if there were not enough problems involved in trying to enforce a law that so many people were determined to disobey, the enforcement agency itself was inept. There had never been an organized system of screening and hiring Prohibition agents. Most of them got their jobs through political influence, and they were often as dishonest as the bootleggers they were hired to track down. Some, in fact, were bootleggers themselves. Others worked with bootleggers, helping them get permits to buy industrial alcohol and tipping them off when raids were planned.

A Prohibition agent's salary averaged less than three thousand dollars a year, yet many of them drove expensive cars and owned sumptuous homes, bought with the money they made from bribes.

86

Prohibition agents James Coppinger and Edward Kelly in normal attire. Below, the same two in disguise for a raid at Lynn, Massachusetts, 1921.

Police and public officials who were supposed to enforce the Volstead Act at the local level were often corrupt, too. In one town in Florida, the mayor, the chief of police, the head of the city council, and the fire commissioner were indicted for Prohibition violations. Elsewhere, judges, sheriffs, and county prosecutors were arrested. In Massachusetts a conscientious Prohibition agent raided a political banquet where liquor was being served. His own boss turned out to be among the guests, and the agent was fired for his trouble.

Two of the best known and most honest Prohibition agents were Izzy Einstein and Moe Smith. They were both short and fat and made a highly unlikely-looking pair of sleuths, but together they seized more than fifteen million dollars' worth of illegal liquor, raided thousands of stills and speakeasies, and made over four thousand arrests.

Izzy spoke eight or nine languages, which made it easy for him to put on almost any disguise. Once, however, he got into a speakeasy simply by identifying himself as a Prohibition agent. The bartender thought he was kidding until Izzy arrested him. On another occasion, Izzy posed as a rabbi and tried to buy sacramental wine from a genuine rabbi who was selling it illegally. The rabbi refused to deal with Einstein because he didn't look Jewish. Izzy finally had to send another agent, Dennis J. Donovan, around to buy the wine and make the arrest.

Although they were pitted against some of the toughest criminals in the country, Izzy and Moe relied only on their wits and their fists. Izzy was afraid of guns and refused to carry one, and Moe used his revolver only twice—once to shoot open a padlock and once to demolish a keg of whiskey.

Izzy Einstein and Moe Smith put more bootleggers out of business than any other agents in the Prohibition Bureau. The newspapers loved the crazy tricks they used to carry out their raids, and they were frequently in the headlines. This irritated their superiors at the Prohibition Bureau. They decided that dignity was more important than honesty or efficiency, and Izzy and Moe were asked to resign.

The adoption of the Eighteenth Amendment led to a host of problems that neither wets nor drys had anticipated. Gun battles erupted between bootleggers and Prohibition agents and there were a number of deaths on both sides. In addition, neither the courts nor the prisons were equipped to cope with the enormous number of people who were arrested for Prohibition violations. In three years the population of the federal prisons almost doubled, and the courts were saddled with some twenty-five thousand more cases than they could handle each year.

The most disastrous result of Prohibition, however, was its impact on the growth of organized crime. Racketeers and gangsters were not a new phenomenon on the American scene, but Prohibition gave them a chance to make vast sums of money and to develop a well-organized system for carrying out their illegal activities. Gangsters like Al Capone and "Legs" Diamond headed huge syndicates that not only made and sold bootleg liquor but also owned speakeasies and nightclubs. Rival gangsters who tried to muscle in on their business were gunned down or disappeared under mysterious circumstances.

In the beginning, many people were fascinated rather than horrified by the way the gangsters operated. Al Capone wore flashy clothes and went around handing out fifty-dollar tips to newsboys and hatcheck girls. But the public's fascination with gangsters declined sharply after the St. Valentine's Day Massacre on February 14, 1929.

Seven hoods were waiting for an illegal shipment of liquor in a garage on Chicago's North Side when a car stopped outside and five men dressed like policemen stepped out. The men, who belonged to another gang of bootleggers, walked into the garage, machine-gunned all

Al Capone, well-known bootlegger and gangster.

seven of their rivals, and drove off. The brutal and cold-blooded slaying made the public think twice not only about gangsters but also about the constitutional amendment that had unleashed such violence and lawlessness. The incident contributed to the steadily mounting revulsion against Prohibition.

Oddly enough, when the clamor for the Eighteenth Amendment was in full force, only the whiskey distillers and brewers, whose livelihood was at stake, had made any serious attempt to fight it. After the amendment was ratified there were brief flurries of protest—marches and demonstrations in Baltimore, New York, and Washington —but they soon died down. Many people disliked Prohibition, but for a long time they seemed resigned to either putting up with it or ignoring it. Then slowly a reaction began to set in. Several small organizations were formed, including the Association Against Prohibition, the Crusaders, the Moderation League, and the Constitutional

Liberty League of Massachusetts. They won national attention in 1926 when they joined forces with the American Federation of Labor and presented the case against Prohibition before a congressional committee investigating its enforcement.

In the course of the next few years several labor unions spoke out for repeal of the Eighteenth Amendment, and a number of lawyers' organizations added their voices to the swelling chorus. The lawyers saw the amendment as a violation of the personal liberties guaranteed by the Bill of Rights, and in 1930 the American Bar Association adopted a resolution calling for its repeal.

Despite the country's disillusionment, any hope of repeal

A view of the St. Valentine's Day Massacre in Chicago, Illinois, 1929.

seemed as futile as Prohibition had seemed a dozen years before. The man who had originally proposed the Eighteenth Amendment, Senator Morris Sheppard of Texas, said there was as much chance of revoking the law as there was "for a hummingbird to fly to the planet Mars with the Washington Monument tied to its tail."

As time went on, however, the feeling against the amendment grew even stronger. A number of prominent businessmen, educators, and authors joined the ranks of the Anti-Prohibitionists; a group of women formed the Women's Organization for National Prohibition Reform and joined in the demands for repeal. At the same time, the power of the temperance movement waned. Once their objective had been attained, people stopped contributing to the cause, so there was little money to finance a campaign against repeal. In addition, the drys were hard put to defend Prohibition because whenever they did, they found themselves defending bootleggers, gangsters, and speakeasies.

Alfred E. Smith, the Catholic governor of New York, was an avowed wet. When he became the Democratic nominee for the presidency in 1928, he made one of the first gestures toward softening the government's stand against alcohol. Among his campaign promises was a pledge to modify the Volstead Act to allow individual states to make their own decisions about Prohibition and its enforcement. Smith's position outraged a Methodist Bishop, James Cannon, Jr., a prominent Prohibitionist and longtime Democrat. Cannon withdrew his support from the Democrats and campaigned for the Republican candidate, Herbert Hoover. He also launched a hate campaign against Smith, spreading vicious anti-Catholic rumors that helped contribute to his defeat.

By the time the next presidential election rolled around in 1932, the United States was thoroughly disgusted with Prohibition. By now the country was in the throes of the

Poster as Al Smith's supporters saw themselves, 1928.

Great Depression, and it was easy to argue that it had been brought on by Prohibition. It was also easy to point out that repeal would provide sorely needed jobs in the liquor industry and that whiskey taxes would add extra money to the dwindling federal Treasury. Just as the emotional climate created by World War I helped bring on the adoption of the Eighteenth Amendment, the emotional climate created by the Great Depression helped speed its repeal.

During his campaign for reelection in 1932, Herbert Hoover referred to Prohibition as an "experiment noble in purpose." He conceded, however, that the experiment had its shortcomings and promised to do what he could to correct them. His Democratic opponent, Franklin D. Roosevelt, was more explicit. "I promise you," he told the convention that nominated him, "that from this date on, the Eighteenth Amendment is doomed!"

There were many reasons why Franklin D. Roosevelt

Governor Franklin D. Roosevelt acknowledging the cheers of 12,000 in the Boston Arena, Boston, Massachusetts, October 31, 1932. At the left is Mayor James M. Curley of Boston, and at the right, behind the first microphone, is Governor Joseph B. Ely of Massachusetts.

defeated Herbert Hoover that November, but Roosevelt's promise to repeal the Eighteenth Amendment was undoubtedly among them. The newly elected president lost no time in fulfilling his promise. Nine days after his inauguration in March, 1933, he asked Congress to amend the Volstead Act so the alcoholic content of beer could be raised from 0.5 percent to 3.2 percent. Congress immediately passed the law, and it went into effect on April 7. Even before that, however, both houses of Congress had passed a resolution submitting a Twenty-first Amendment to the Constitution to the states for ratification. It would repeal the Eighteenth Amendment and return to the states the right to make their own liquor laws.

The dry forces, which less than two decades before had

Kegs of beer for the thirsty in New York's bright light district—unloading beer in front of a well-known restaurant on Broadway, the morning of April 7, 1933, the day the Prohibition Amendment was repealed.

been a major political force, now murmured only faint cries of protest. A year after Roosevelt's election the required number of states had ratified the Twenty-first Amendment, and on December 5, 1933, it became part of the United States Constitution. The Noble Experiment was over, and the whole country breathed a loud sigh of relief.

Since the repeal of the Eighteenth Amendment alcohol has played a less prominent, but no less pervasive, role in American life. In most parts of the country, drinking is an accepted part of the culture. The making, selling, and importing of liquor is a lucrative business, and both our federal and state governments derive a substantial income from the taxes on it.

ALCOHOL: The Delightful Poison

In the centuries since its discovery alcohol has played a part in economics, politics, religion, and history, but its most important role, its influence on men's personal lives, is, in many ways, still a mystery.

PART III

MYTH AND TRUTH

The Mystery of Alcoholism

Man no sooner discovered drinking than he also discovered drunkenness. Overdrinking was common in Egypt, and although the Greeks and the Romans added water to their wine to reduce its strength, people got drunk there, too.

The Greek city-state of Sparta had strict moral and physical standards. The Spartans frowned on excessive drinking and made their slaves get drunk in front of their children so the children could see how foolish drunkards were. The Roman writer and philosopher, Seneca, shared the Spartans' view of overdrinking. "Drunkenness," he wrote, "is simply voluntary insanity."

The Hebrews enjoyed wine, but possibly because of the excesses they had seen during their long captivity in Egypt, had no use for drunkards. The Old Testament has a number of warnings against overindulgence in alcohol. The Book of Isaiah promises, "Woe unto them that rise up early in the morning, that they may follow strong drink." The Book of Joel says, "Awake, ye drunkards and weep; and howl, all ye drinkers of wine." To this day, drunkenness is rare among Jews, and many Jewish people never drink anything except the ritual wine at their Seders.

ALCOHOL: The Delightful Poison

Although an Arab gave the world the technique for distilling alcohol, Arabs are forbidden by the Muslim religion to drink anything alcoholic. The prophet Muhammad, who founded the Muslim faith in the 7th century, was a firm believer in abstinence. "The devil desires to sow dissensions and hatred among you through wine and games of chance," he wrote in the Koran, "be obedient to God and the prophet, his apostle, and take heed to yourselves."

Several explanations have been given for Muhammad's stern opposition to alcohol. Some historians say that drunkenness was once quite common among the Arabs, and Muhammad saw his new religion as a chance to effect some much needed reforms. Others say that on one occasion when the prophet's armies were engaged in one of their many wars, several of his officers got drunk and fell to quarreling among themselves. This destroyed discipline among the troops and almost cost them an important battle. After this Muhammad forbade the use of intoxicating beverages by his followers.

In the past a few philosophers and religious leaders realized the dangers of too much drinking and urged people to avoid it, but for the most part, drunkenness was accepted as an unavoidable, but not particularly serious, consequence of drinking. The 13th-century Mongol conqueror, Genghis Khan, typified the general attitude. "A soldier must not get drunk oftener than once a week," he said. "It would, of course, be better if he did not get drunk at all, but one should not expect the impossible."

A few countries had laws about drinking, but they were designed to protect drinkers from unscrupulous merchants by regulating the quantity and quality of the drinks that were sold. It was not until the 15th century that it finally dawned on the lawmakers that drinkers also needed to be protected from themselves.

England, where drinking was an extraordinarily popular

diversion, was the first country to realize that controls were necessary. In 1495 English judges were given the right to regulate the number of ale or "tippling" houses in each town. A few decades later, another law was passed, stipulating that alehouse keepers must buy a license to sell ale. The licensing fee was designed to cut down on the number of alehouses and to enable the government to withhold licenses from ale sellers who were apt to become as drunk and disorderly as their patrons.

In spite of these measures, excessive drinking continued to be a nuisance, and a new set of laws was passed. Staying too long in an alehouse became a punishable offense, and innkeepers were forbidden to serve drinks to anyone but travelers, guests, and laboring men at their dinner hour. Illegal alehouses, where the laws were ignored, soon opened up, and still another law was necessary. It provided that anyone keeping an illegal alehouse was to be punished by flogging.

Drunkenness persisted, and Parliament finally turned its attention from the ale sellers to the ale drinkers. Between 1604 and 1627 more than half a dozen laws were passed against drunkards. A person who was caught drinking too much was fined, and the fine was donated to the poor. Anyone who could not pay it was placed in the stocks. People caught tippling on Sunday when church services were in progress were also put in the stocks. In many places churchwardens regularly made the rounds of all the alehouses in the parish, hoping to catch such culprits.

Another punishment that was sometimes meted out in lieu of the stocks was the "drunkard's coat." This was a large wooden barrel with a hole at the top for the head and one on each side for the arms. Drunkards were forced to wear it in public and would supposedly be so mortified that they would never get drunk again.

Despite the various laws and punishments against excessive drinking, drunkenness showed no signs of declining.

In the seventeenth century, drunks were often put in the stocks, as seen in this engraving by J. Romney from a painting by William Hogarth.

It was a problem when ale was the principal drink in England. It became an even worse problem after English soldiers fought several wars in the Netherlands during the 17th century and returned home with a taste for brandy and gin. Around this same time, another event occurred that helped bring about a major change in England's drinking habits.

In 1643 Parliament voted to place a tax on ale and beer. Over the course of the next few years the tax was raised several times, and by 1690 it was so high that people could no longer afford to drink beer. They began looking for a cheaper substitute, and the government helped them find it. At that time England was encouraging

Cartoon showing the drunkard's cloak in Elizabethan England.

farmers to raise grain. As a result of their efforts the countryside was lined with grain fields. The crops provided the raw material for a cheaper and far more potent drink than ale—gin.

Gin making, selling, and drinking quickly became England's major pastimes. Candlemakers and butchers stocked gin on their shelves. Gin shops opened on every corner with signs over their doors claiming: "Here a man may get drunk for a penny, and dead drunk for twopence." Street vendors set up stands wherever they could find customers. In no time at all, England was in the throes of "Gin Fever." Robberies, murders, and brawls increased, thousands died from overdrinking, thousands more were constantly drunk and unable to work.

The satirical artist William Hogarth gave a good, and probably not too exaggerated, picture of the situation in his print, "Gin Lane." The engraving shows a group of befuddled, shabbily dressed gin drinkers, including a woman who is so drunk that her baby is slipping from her arms. The only sober and prosperous-looking man in the picture is the undertaker.

As soon as the English government realized the disastrous results of its gin policy, Parliament promptly set about trying to remedy the situation. The Gin Act, which was passed in 1736, put a tax on gin, required that gin shops be licensed, and forbade the sale of gin in quantities smaller than a gallon, on the assumption that the average person could not afford to pay for that much gin.

When the new act went into effect, England's gin shops were draped in black and in some places there were gin riots. The protests proved unnecessary because every effort was made to circumvent the law. Shopkeepers pretending to be druggists sold "cholick water" to ward off disease, street vendors took to selling a mysterious "mixture," and a few gin makers added spices and sugar to their gin and sold it as wine.

It was over two centuries before Gin Fever finally died out. During that time, the consumption of all kinds of alcohol increased and England became known as "a nation of drunkards." Gentlemen were proud of the fact that they could drink two bottles of wine at a sitting, and at dinner parties both men and women regularly drank until they slid under the table. The 17th-century philosopher Thomas Hobbes, who considered himself a temperate man, boasted that he had "not been drunk above a hundred times" in his life.

The English, as one wit put it, had become a people "who drink everyone else's health to impair their own." A chief justice of the 17th century was so alarmed by the trend that he ordered his grandchildren not to follow the custom of drinking healths.

"I will not have you to begin or pledge any health," he wrote in his will, "for it is becoming one of the great artifices of drinking and occasions of quarrelling in the kingdom. If you pledge one health, you oblige yourself to pledge another, and a third, and so onwards; and if you pledge as many as will be drank, you must be debauched and drunk. If they will needs know the reason of your refusal, it is a fair answer, That your grandfather that

Eighteenth-century British print of the painting "Gin Lane" by William Hogarth.

brought you up, from whom under God you have the estate you enjoy or expect, left this in command with you, that you should never begin or pledge a health." Parliament tried over a period of several decades to correct the abuses caused by its original gin policy, but it was not until 1839, when it became cheaper to get a license to sell beer, that beer shops replaced gin shops and ale was restored to its former place as England's favorite drink.

Although Gin Fever never reached the thirteen colonies, excessive drinking was a fact of life in America, too. George Washington issued a daily ration of rum to his troops, but he also issued strict orders against drunkenness.

After the Revolution, Washington encouraged trade with France in hopes of persuading his fellow countrymen to drink wine, which, he said, "would at least be more innocent to the health and morals of the people than the thousands of Hogsheads of poisonous Rum which are annually consumed in the United States."

The French cooperated with Washington's efforts to encourage wine drinking. Shortly after the Revolution the French consul in Boston invited a group of prominent citizens to a champagne party. The Bostonians, thinking they were sampling a new type of sparkling cider, got thoroughly drunk but were not otherwise impressed with the drink.

Thomas Jefferson was also concerned about the American appetite for alcohol. During his presidency Jefferson invited a group of Bohemian brewers to come to the United States to help train Americans in the art of making beer. "I wish to see this beverage become common instead of the whiskey which kills one third of our citizens and ruins their families," he wrote to a friend in 1815.

Beer drinking did not become as common as Jefferson had hoped, and he turned his attention to promoting the use of his own favorite beverage, wine. "No nation is drunken where wine is cheap," he wrote to a French friend in 1818, "and none sober where the dearness of wine substitutes ardent spirits as the common beverage. It is, in truth, the only antidote to the bane of whiskey."

Fine sherry and Madeira had long been served in the homes of upper-class Americans, but the average citizen, who did most of his drinking in taverns, was more apt to order whiskey or, until the collapse of the slave trade, rum. Brandy, gin, and hard cider were also available and sold for astoundingly low prices. In a typical year, 1838, beer cost only six cents a quart, and whiskey, about thirty-eight cents a gallon.

In his 1784 treatise against alcohol, Dr. Benjamin Rush had suggested putting heavy taxes on "ardent spirits" to make them more difficult to buy. The federal government passed one tax on whiskey in 1794. Another was added a few years later to help pay for the War of 1812, and still another in 1862 to raise money for the Civil War. Individual states levied taxes of their own, but even with higher prices drunkenness remained as much of a problem as it had been in the days when liquor sold for only a few pennies.

The temperance leaders thought they had a solution to drunkenness. They considered it a sin and believed that drunkards could reform if they would only go to church regularly and exercise a little self-control. When prayers and preaching failed, the teetotalers turned to Prohibition, which proved to be the most spectacular failure of all.

The country's attitude toward drunkenness was no more enlightened than the teetotalers'. For a long time the problem was left in the hands of the clergy or the police. Then, gradually, a few medical men began to suspect that overdrinking might not be a sin or a crime but a disease. In 1828 a Connecticut doctor, Eli Todd, superintendent of the Hartford Retreat for the Insane, suggested setting up a hospital for the care and treatment of drunk-ards. Todd's suggestion met with stony silence from his colleagues. In 1864 another doctor, J. Edward Turner, established an Inebriate Asylum in Binghamton, New York. The protests from the clergy and from Turner's fellow doctors were so vehement that he was forced to close it down.

The country's first and, for years, only hospital for chronic drinkers, the Washingtonian Home for the Fallen, was founded in Boston in 1868. The use of the word *fallen* was an attempt to foster a more sympathetic attitude toward drunkards. Another concerned physician, Dr. Magnus Huss, suggested replacing the word *drunkard* with *alcoholic*, but it was more than fifty years before the term came into general use. These initial efforts to understand and treat problem drinkers met with little success. Most people continued to regard drunkenness as a moral failure.

The development of psychiatry in Europe during the latter part of the 19th century made doctors realize that there were many different types of illness besides the fevers and infections they usually treated. When psychiatry spread to the United States, the idea that alcoholism was a disease gradually became more acceptable, but doctors were still at a loss to explain its causes or prescribe a cure.

In 1842 the German scientist Justus von Liebig made the first studies of how the body disposes of alcohol. Further research was later undertaken into other aspects of alcohol's effect on the human body, but none of the findings offered any clues to the mystery of alcoholism.

The first scientific studies of alcoholism did not begin in the United States until 1930. They were inspired, ironically, by Prohibition. Doctors, alarmed by the tremendous increase in excessive drinking throughout the country, decided to take a closer look at the problem. The Laboratory of Applied Physiology at Yale University launched the first investigation into the riddle of alcoholism. Since then, other research centers have been established. Their staffs include not only doctors but sociologists, biochemists, psychologists, and geneticists.

Although scientists now know much more about alcohol than they did in the past, many questions about alcoholism remain unanswered. The first and most important is why some people become alcoholics and others don't. One widely accepted theory is that the alcoholic has some type of basic personality disorder that compels him to seek escape in alcohol. Other researchers suspect that alcoholism is a physical, rather than an emotional, problem and that alcoholics may have some factor in their body chemistry that predisposes them to the disease.

One thing the scientists do know is that there are large numbers of people who, because of either their physical or emotional makeup, will never become alcoholics. Some are sensitive to alcohol and become dizzy or nauseous after a single drink. Others simply don't like the feeling of relaxation and release that alcohol gives them. Research has also shown that the culture a person lives in can be a factor in whether or not he becomes an alcoholic. Without exception alcoholics have been brought up in an environment where drinking is socially acceptable and where alcohol is used freely and often.

Since the causes of alcoholism are still unknown, doctors are at a loss to know how to treat it. They have experimented with varying degrees of success with several methods. One is a drug called Antabuse, which creates an aversion for alcohol by producing a variety of unpleasant symptoms, such as hot flashes, headache, and difficulty in breathing, whenever the user takes a drink. Psychotherapy with a psychiatrist, psychologist, or social worker has worked for some alcoholics, helping them to understand the reasons for their drinking and to solve the problems it has caused in their lives.

To date the most effective method that has been discovered for dealing with alcoholism is an organization called Alcoholics Anonymous. Founded in 1935 by two former alcoholics, a New York stockbroker and an Ohio doctor, AA currently has about five hundred thousand members organized in small chapters around the country. They meet regularly to exchange stories of their experiences with alcohol and to offer encouragement and support to other alcoholics who are trying to give up drinking.

AA is really a form of group therapy. It pledges its members to total abstinence and urges them to place their trust in God. Some people have criticized the organization for its strong religious outlook and for its insistence on total abstinence, but most experts on alcoholism support AA, if only because it has produced such good results.

It has been estimated that about ten million Americans have serious drinking problems. Research into alcohol and alcoholism has already helped some of them and may eventually help many more. Such research is equally important for the millions of other Americans who are not problem drinkers. Only by understanding what alcohol is and how it works can they decide whether to drink or not, and if they do drink, learn to do it without harm to themselves or anyone else.

⑨

Myths and Mistakes

For the first few thousand years of its existence, alcohol was regarded not only as a precious gift, but as a boon to life and health.

The Ebers papyrus, which served as a handbook for the pharmacists of ancient Egypt, contained the ingredients for a long list of medicines. Of the seven hundred prescriptions included in the document, one hundred were made with beer. The Anglo-Saxons also had great confidence in the healing powers of beer. They used it for coughs and shortness of breath and for curing the hiccups. Ale was recommended for rubbing on the knees to relieve aches and pains.

Greek and Roman physicians regularly prescribed wine for their patients. They gave it to soothe the spirit, revive the heart, and alleviate pain. The Jews and early Christians also used alcohol as medicine. In one of his epistles to Timothy, St. Paul advised, "Use a little wine for thy stomach's sake and thine other infirmities." Centuries later, pious Christians still referred to alcohol as "the good creature of God," a phrase adapted from St. Paul meaning that alcohol was one of God's gifts and was meant to be enjoyed.

The idea that drinking cured disease and promoted health became even more widespread in the 13th century after Arnauld de Villeneuve pronounced alcohol "the water of life." Physicians all over Europe were soon urging people to drink as much and as often as they liked.

Hieronymus Brunschwig, a highly respected German doctor of the 15th century, called aqua vitae "the mistress of all medicines." Brunschwig saw no end to the problems it could alleviate. In one of his treatises on medicine, he stated:

> It eases the diseases coming of cold, it comforts the heart. It heals all old and new sores on the head. It causes a good color in a person. It heals alopecia [baldness] and causes the hair well to grow, and kills lice and fleas. It cures lethargy. Cotton wet in the same and a little wrung out again and so put in the ears at night going to bed, and a little drunk thereof, is of good against all deafness.

Aqua vitae enjoyed its reputation as a universal cure-all for several centuries. Even after it ceased to be regarded as the answer to every medical problem, it was still seen as the answer to most of them. This tradition carried over to America, where for a long while, anyone who wanted to stay healthy always started the day with a glass of "bitters." Liquor was recommended for people of all ages and administered for every imaginable condition. Cranky babies were lulled to sleep with rum and water. Children were dosed with blackberry brandy for stomachaches. Older people sipped beer to ease the pain of rheumatism and arthritis.

Alcohol was also expected to prevent disease. Churches and taverns were built side by side so colonial worshipers could adjourn for hot toddies midway through the services and thus keep from catching cold in the unheated churches. Many early Americans drank as a protection against malaria and typhoid fever. Considering the sanitary conditions of the times, alcohol was probably a safer thirst quencher than water, but this hardly justified the quantities in which it was consumed.

During the 19th century alcohol was widely used as a remedy for snakebite. The idea that alcohol could counteract snake venom in the human body started in the 2nd century B.C. The Greek poet Nicander advised drinking large amounts of wine as quickly as possible after being bitten. His theory was that the alcohol would neutralize the snake venom, but if it was not taken at once, the snake venom would take over and the victim would die.

Nicander's remedy was revived on the American frontier where rattlesnake bites were a common occurrence. The frontier doctors prescribed 100-proof whiskey instead of wine and ordered a full quart to be taken within twelve hours of the attack. If the victim was alive, but still not recovering, after the first twelve hours more whiskey was called for. An article in the *North-West Medical Surgical Journal* in 1855 described one man who downed six quarts of whiskey and a bottle of brandy before he finally rallied.

Until the discovery of ether in 1846, alcohol was widely used to dull the pain of tooth extractions and surgery. Even when it was no longer used as an anesthetic, its reputation as a healer was slow to die out. In 1900 Sir William Osler, the most brilliant physician of his era, called alcohol "our most valuable medicinal agent." In Osler's day hospitals kept whiskey, beer, and brandy on their medicine shelves. They called them "stimulants" and doled them out to patients two or three times a day. Doctors ordered stimulants for practically everything—relieving pain, preventing infection after childbirth, and reviving victims of shock. They were also given after surgery and for heart and respiratory diseases.

Even during Prohibition, doctors were allowed to prescribe, and druggists to sell, up to one quart of whiskey per patient per month for medicinal purposes. By then, however, the practice of prescribing alcohol was already on the wane. Doctors were beginning to suspect that it was of little value in most medical situations and in some cases might even be hindering their patients' recovery. Their suspicions were subsequently confirmed by medical research.

Although modern doctors rarely prescribe alcohol for anything, there are still some laymen who are convinced that it is the only antidote for conditions like shock and prolonged exposure to cold. It can in fact be dangerous in both situations. Shock victims suffer a sharp drop in blood pressure, and alcohol only lowers the blood pressure still further. People suffering from chills and frostbite are not helped by drinking, either. Although it appears to warm the body, alcohol actually contributes to a further loss of heat. Whiskey's reputation as a remedy for coughs and colds is also undeserved, although it may temporarily relieve their discomforts by making the sufferers relax and forget about them.

This ability to make people relax is often cited as one of alcohol's greatest benefits. It is one of its prime dangers as well. People who drink to reduce their tensions can become psychologically dependent on alcohol and can also develop a tolerance for it. This means that they find themselves unable to function in social or business situations without a drink and that, as time goes on, they need increasingly greater amounts to produce the same effect.

Alcohol has a reputation for making people more sociable, but it is not always deserved. Alcohol does reduce inhibitions, but by doing so it may reveal that a person is really hostile and quarrelsome. Nor will alcohol, as some drinkers claim, help them to function more efficiently. It only causes them to be less embarrassed when they make mistakes.

Sanatogen—Restorer of Exhausted Nerves

FEW men and women escape trouble with their nerves—many suffer, perhaps to the verge of complete breakdown, without knowing the true reason.

The warning appears in sleeplessness, in loss of appetite, disturbed digestion, weakened powers of body and mind, in "low spirits" that are all too seldom attributed to their actual cause—impoverishment of nerves and tissues.

Sanatogen recognizes the true nature of these conditions and *scientifically meets them.* Sanatogen carries to these nerves and tissues the *tonic food* demanded by their exhausted state—the particular *natural* nourishment quickly and eagerly assimilated by the starved centres. The system rejoices in getting the specific food it has needed, and an aroused and *sustained* vitality is shown in the return of new power, new buoyancy, new courage and efficiency.

If *you* feel the need of bodily renewal, consider seriously the remarkable fact that 15,000 practising physicians have enthusiastically endorsed the *reconstructive*, rejuvenating power of Sanatogen.

A Remarkable Book FREE upon request

We ask you earnestly to get acquainted with Sanatogen. Investigate our claims first if you like and we are only too glad to have you do so. Ask your doctor about it, and in any case write at once for our book "Our Nerves of Tomorrow," written in an absorbingly interesting style, beautifully illustrated and containing facts and information of vital interest to you. This book also contains evidence of the value of Sanatogen which is as remarkable as it is conclusive.

Sanatogen is sold in three sizes, $1.00, $1.90, $3.60

Get Sanatogen from your druggist—if not obtainable from him, sent upon receipt of price.

THE BAUER CHEMICAL CO. 45 East Seventeenth Street Union Square, New York

David Belasco
The eminent dramatic author, writes:
"It gives me pleasure to let you know the wonderfully beneficial results I have experienced from the use of your Sanatogen. It has a most invigorating effect upon the nerves and I heartily recommend it to all those who, like myself, are obliged to overwork. After my personal experience I can readily vouch for its recuperating qualities."

Hall Caine
The dramatist, writes:
"My experience of Sanatogen has been that as a tonic nerve food it has on more than one occasion benefited me."

Sir Gilbert Parker, M.P.
The eminent novelist statesman, writes from London:
"Sanatogen is to my mind a true food-tonic, feeding the nerves, increasing the energy and giving fresh vigor to the overworked body and mind."

George Ade
The humorist, writes:
"I have given Sanatogen a trial and I am convinced of its merits."

Mme. Sarah Grand
Author of the "Heavenly Twins," writes:
"I began to take Sanatogen after nearly four years' enforced idleness from extreme debility, and felt the benefit almost immediately. And now, after taking it steadily three times a day for twelve weeks, I find myself able to enjoy both work and play again and also am able to do as much of both as I ever did."

Advertisement for Sanatogen, "Restorer of Exhausted Nerves," one of the many patent medicines of the late nineteenth century. Often such remedies contained up to 80% alcohol.

ALCOHOL: The Delightful Poison

One all too common misconception about drinking is that it is a smart or sophisticated thing to do. This is totally false. Many smart and sophisticated people do not drink at all, others drink only occasionally or take no more than a little wine with their meals. Whether a person drinks or not is a matter of personal preference, and it is nobody's business but his own. It is definitely not a subject for teasing or questions or, for that matter, for any comment at all.

While the benefits of alcohol have often been misunderstood and exaggerated, its dangers have also been gravely misrepresented. The misrepresentations began with the rise of the temperance movement and stemmed from a combination of scientific ignorance and a deliberate desire to mislead.

Perhaps the most ridiculous of the many accusations against alcohol was the charge that it could cause people to catch fire. Dr. Benjamin Rush told the supposedly true tale of a drunkard who belched near a candle flame and was "suddenly destroyed." Other medical men substantiated Rush's story, and the idea that chronic drinkers could abruptly burst into flames became fairly prevalent. One of the characters in the temperance play *Ten Nights in a Bar-Room* says that he doesn't like to spend too much time with the tavern owner because he is "afraid of spontaneous combustion."

More plausible, but still untrue, were the stories that alcohol caused such illnesses as cancer, tuberculosis, and heart trouble. As part of their scare tactics, whenever an epidemic of typhoid or cholera occurred, temperance leaders hastened to assure the public that people who drank would be among the first to fall ill.

Among the other myths that were perpetrated in the name of temperance was the idea that alcohol caused epilepsy, idiocy, and insanity. Even worse was the belief that people who drank would pass these conditions on to their children. A physiology book prepared for school-children by the Women's Christian Temperance Union declared, "Many men and women are insane because they inherit disordered bodies and minds, caused by the drinking habits of their parents."

Another totally unfounded assertion was that the desire for drink was an inherited trait. On this assumption the descendants of drinkers had only to take a small sip of brandy or sample a jelly flavored with wine and they would be addicted to alcohol for the rest of their lives.

An amusing, but in some cases tragic, sidelight to the teetotalers' disdain for alcohol was that many of them had no qualms about using the various patent medicines that sold so widely in the latter part of the 19th century. The mixtures, guaranteed to cure everything from corns to kidney stones, were of dubious medicinal value, and many of them contained as much as 80 percent alcohol.

Patent medicines turned many unsuspecting users into chronic drunkards. The companies that made them were eventually exposed by muckraking journalists, and in 1906 Congress passed the Pure Food and Drug Act, which gave the federal government the right to regulate the contents of medicines and the claims that could be made for them.

With the decline of the temperance movement most of the myths and mistakes about alcohol were safely laid to rest. Even today, however, the idea that drinking is physically harmful is not completely dead. Many otherwise well-informed people still do not understand its effect on the human body.

It is true that heavy drinkers are more apt to contract certain diseases, but these illnesses are associated with, not caused by, alcohol. Chronic drinkers, for example, are more susceptible to stomach disorders, circulatory problems, and respiratory infections such as lobar pneumonia. Many of them also suffer from a skin condition called acne

rosacea in which the blood vessels in the face, and particularly the nose, become enlarged and red.

Since alcohol provides energy but not nourishment, drinkers often neglect to eat. As a result they become undernourished, and this makes them more prone to illness. The disease that is most commonly attributed to overdrinking, cirrhosis of the liver, is usually caused by a nutritional deficiency. Like the other illnesses associated with alcohol, it can occur among nondrinkers as well as drinkers.

Alcohol can aggravate existing problems like gout, ulcers, hepatitis, and epilepsy, but the only disease that it actually causes is alcoholism. Once a person becomes an alcoholic, however, he or she may develop several disabling and sometimes fatal diseases of the brain, nerves, and liver. The alcoholic is also subject to another agonizing condition, delirium tremens, or the D.T.'s, which usually occurs when a heavy drinker is deprived of alcohol. The symptoms of the D.T.'s are mental confusion, fits of violent shaking, and hallucinations that include visions of rats and snakes or ants crawling under the skin. Its victims often die of heart failure or suffer permanent brain damage from alcohol poisoning.

Throughout history human beings have tried to find a way to drink as much as they liked without getting drunk. Their ideas for achieving this impossible dream have, if nothing else, been highly imaginative.

The Chinese believed that a precious stone held under the tongue would do the trick. For a while the Romans also believed in a precious stone, the amethyst, but they used it to adorn their wine goblets. Various foods were also thought to possess magical properties. The Egyptians ate boiled cabbage leaves when they drank, and the Romans, during the reign of Tiberius, chewed bitter almonds. Just as imaginative and equally useless were the cures for the aftereffects of drinking. The Chinese recommended fish soup; the English preferred stork eggs and "little greene frogges." More recently, sauerkraut juice and yogurt have had their day.

Remedies for chronic drunkenness have also been eagerly sought after. A formula that was popular in Russia during the 12th century was to conceal a piece of pork in a Jew's bed for nine days. The pork was then mashed up and given to the drunkard, who would supposedly avoid alcohol as faithfully as Jews avoided pork. In the United States during the 1880's Dr. Leslie E. Keeley, a Dwight, Illinois, physician, made a small fortune claiming to cure alcoholics with a mixture of gold and water that he advertised widely as the "Keeley Cure."

Of all the myths that have been perpetrated about alcohol, probably the most dangerous is the idea that drinking is a joke. The drunk who slurs his words, staggers about and falls on his face, has always been good for a laugh in the entertainment business, and too often in real life.

Alcoholism is a serious and tragic affliction. It ranks with cancer, heart disease, and mental illness as one of the major health problems confronting the United States. No one would dream of laughing at someone with cancer or schizophrenia, yet most people see no harm in making jokes about people who drink too much. If the myths and mistakes about alcohol are ever completely banished, the idea that it is a laughing matter ought to be among the first to go.

10

The Sober
Truth

For many years alcohol was regarded in the medical profession as both a food and a stimulant. Today, doctors know that it is neither. Ethyl alcohol is now classified as a drug and recognized as a depressant that acts as an anesthetic on the central nervous system.

Alcohol resembles food, because like meat, fruits, and vegetables, it contains calories, or units of energy. Unlike these foods, however, it contains none of the vitamins, minerals, and proteins that provide the body with nourishment.

Alcohol is similar to food in another respect—it undergoes the same chemical process in the human body. The process, oxidation, occurs when the oxygen in the body combines with a substance, burns off its original chemical ingredients, and reduces it to carbon dioxide and water. Between 90 and 98 percent of the alcohol taken into the human body is destroyed through oxidation. The remaining 2 to 10 percent is excreted through the lungs as breath, through the kidneys as urine, or in lesser amounts, through other bodily fluids such as tears, sweat, bile, or stomach juices.

Most foods are oxidized slowly at successive stages of

the digestive process. Alcohol begins to oxidize at once, and the oxidation occurs mainly in the liver. When a person takes a drink, the alcohol is absorbed virtually unchanged into the stomach and small intestine. From there it is carried by the blood to the liver.

The average liver can oxidize one-half ounce of alcohol per hour, or about one or two drops per minute. Therefore, even though the oxidation process begins within a few seconds after the alcohol reaches the liver, some unoxidized alcohol inevitably passes into the bloodstream. It is carried to the heart, which then pumps it back through the circulatory system, so it reaches every part of the human body, including the brain.

During the circulatory process, the alcohol continues to return to the liver until it is completely oxidized. The amount of time this takes will depend on how much and how fast a person drinks. One ounce of whiskey sipped slowly over a one-hour period will burn off quickly and produce a low blood-alcohol level. The same amount downed in one gulp will take longer to burn off and will produce a high blood-alcohol level. If a person has had a great deal to drink, it may take eight or ten hours for the alcohol in his blood to burn off.

There is no way to speed up the oxidation process. Black coffee, cold showers, and physical exercise are sometimes given to drinkers to sober them up. Such measures may make them more alert, but they cannot accelerate the rate at which alcohol is metabolized into carbon dioxide. The only thing that can do this is time.

Alcohol is absorbed into the bloodstream within minutes after the drinker takes his first sip. It gives the impression of affecting the body even faster, however, because it dilates the blood vessels in the lining of the mouth and stomach and produces the sensation of instant heat and stimulation. The sensation is only temporary. As soon as the alcohol is ingested into the bloodstream and pumped to the brain, it begins to work as a depressant.

Alcohol first depresses the cerebral cortex, the section of the brain that controls the higher functions of judgment and social restraint. The drinker becomes livelier and talks more freely, which explains why alcohol is so often mistaken for a stimulant. If a person continues to drink faster than the alcohol is burned off in his body, the alcohol will next depress the cerebellum, which controls coordination, balance, vision, and speech.

The drinker will become progressively uninhibited as the cerebral cortex is affected and progressively confused as the cerebellum is reached. If he goes on drinking, the alcohol will eventually affect the medulla oblongata, which controls the respiration, heart, and other vital functions. When the medulla oblongata is depressed, the result may be sleep, stupor, loss of consciousness, and sometimes death.

Death usually occurs when the victim is already suffering from acute alcoholism, but it can also happen when the body is suddenly overwhelmed by more alcohol than it can handle. Drinkers trying to win bets or contests have been known to down a bottle of whiskey or a dozen cocktails without stopping. More than a few of them have dropped dead as a result. There have also been cases where young children, whose bodies can absorb only a small amount of alcohol, have died after drinking a single glass of whiskey or wine.

A person who has had too much to drink can be placed in one of three categories. He may be under the influence of alcohol, suffering from alcohol intoxication, or a victim of alcohol poisoning. For legal purposes the categories are often differentiated by the concentration of alcohol in the blood. This is not a completely accurate measurement because individual reactions to alcohol vary. As a general rule, however, a person whose blood-alcohol level is between 0.05 and 0.15 percent is considered under the influence. At 0.15 or more, intoxication is present. A blood-alcohol concentration of 0.3 usually produces stupor or sleep, and at 0.4 and above, a person is in a severe state of intoxication and is in danger of death from alcohol poisoning.

What this means in terms of the amount of alcohol consumed is that for someone weighing 150 pounds, the 0.05 level would be reached after slightly less than two highballs or cocktails, three glasses of wine, or four 12-ounce bottles of beer. The 0.15 level would be reached after five highballs or cocktails, 27½ ounces, or slightly less than a quart, of wine, or 10 bottles of beer.

A blood-alcohol concentration of less than 0.05 percent may not legally classify a person as being under the influence of alcohol, but even concentrations of 0.03 percent (which for someone weighing 150 pounds would be after one highball or cocktail, a glass of wine, or two bottles of beer) can produce noticeable effects on behavior. Some drinkers show signs of inattention, poor judgment, and loss of emotional equilibrium. The National Safety Council reports a definite increase in the number of automobile accidents at 0.05 percent.

Several factors can influence the rate at which alcohol is absorbed into the bloodstream. One is the drinker's weight. The average person burns 1/24 of an ounce of alcohol per hour for every 22 pounds of his body weight. Consequently, the person who weighs 200 pounds will burn alcohol faster and have a lower blood-alcohol level after drinking the same amount as a person who weighs half that much.

In addition, different drinks contain different amounts of alcohol. Beer contains 4 percent and wine 12 percent. The alcoholic content of distilled spirits varies depending on their proof. The degree of proof is twice the percentage of alcohol by volume. Hence a 90-proof whiskey contains 45 percent alcohol, and an 86-proof whiskey, 43 percent. The word *proof*, incidentally, dates back to the days when liquor was tested by mixing it with gunpowder. If the liquor contained 50 percent alcohol, the gunpowder would burn. The test was "proof" of its potency.

The rate at which alcohol is absorbed into the bloodstream can be slowed down by diluting it with water. Mixing drinks with ginger ale or soda will, on the other hand, speed up absorption. The carbon dioxide in carbonated drinks hastens the rate at which alcohol passes through the stomach and small intestine and is hurled into the bloodstream. This explains why effervescent wines like champagne and sparkling burgundy have more "kick" than still wines.

Alcohol is also absorbed more slowly when it is mixed with foods like milk, tomato juice, or orange juice, and even more slowly when it is taken with, or just after, a meal. The stomach digests food at a leisurely pace, and the alcohol is delayed in the process. In addition, since the liver is already active and participating in the digestive process, it oxidizes more efficiently. Conversely, alcohol taken on an empty stomach takes the liver by surprise. Oxidation is less efficient, and more alcohol is absorbed into the bloodstream.

There is a popular theory that people who habitually drink large amounts of alcohol absorb it more efficiently and are less likely to become intoxicated. As a matter of actual fact, however, heavy drinkers often have unhealthy livers that burn off alcohol at a slower rate and make them far more susceptible to its effects.

Although some people have a slightly higher tolerance for alcohol than others, anyone who drinks too much has to endure the unpleasant aftereffects known as a hangover. The hangover is a worldwide phenomenon. In France it is called *gueule de bois*, or "mouth of wood"; in Germany *Katzenjammer*, or "the wailing of cats"; and in Norway *jeg har tømmermenn,* meaning, "I have carpenters in my head."

In many instances the misery of a hangover is, at least in part, emotional. There may be feelings of guilt for overindulging in alcohol or embarrassment for things that have been said or done while under its influence. The principal symptoms of a hangover—headache, nausea, fatigue, and thirst—are, however, completely physical.

The headache is induced by the toxic substances in alcohol that have not been completely destroyed by the liver. Nausea occurs because alcohol in large amounts irritates the lining of the stomach. Fatigue is a side effect of the calories in alcohol. The drinker feels stimulated and uses extra energy talking, dancing, or staying up late, without realizing that he is getting overtired.

Hangover thirst is sometimes attributed to the fact that alcohol dehydrates the body. Actually the total amount of water in the body does not change, but some of the water usually contained in the cells shifts to the spaces between them and creates a feeling of dryness. The more a person drinks, the thirstier he will be and the longer it will take for his thirst to disappear.

In addition to the normal reactions to alcohol that everyone experiences, certain drinkers also have a less noticeable but far more dangerous reaction. For some unknown reason, they become dependent on alcohol.

Medically speaking, there are two types of dependence, psychological and physical. Psychological dependence is a common behavioral response. It means that a person has tried something, discovered that it makes him feel good, and wants to try it again. This happens with many drugs. Some people become mildly dependent on the caffeine in coffee, tea, cocoa, or cola drinks. Stronger drugs, like alcohol and nicotine, produce a more severe psychological dependence. The reaction is stronger still with amphetamines, heroin, and cocaine.

Physical dependence on a drug means that certain biochemical changes have taken place in the brain cells that make them unable to function normally unless the drug is present. The physically dependent drug user is an addict who will experience severe withdrawal symptoms if the drug is not taken. This happens with chronic alcoholics who suffer from tremors and hallucinations if they are deprived of a drink for more than a few hours.

In most cases, the shift from moderate drinking to psychological, and then physical, dependence takes place gradually. The first sign of danger occurs when the drinker begins using alcohol as a drug to allay anxieties and help him relax. His drinking is less likely to be done in social situations, and he may discover that his tolerance for alcohol is increasing. In other words, he needs more and more alcohol to make him feel relaxed.

At the next stage, the drinker experiences "blackouts." He seems to function normally while drinking, but afterward he cannot remember what happened. At this point he may be sneaking drinks at all hours of the day and night, usually gulping them down and often taking them straight from the bottle. At the same time, he will deny that he has a drinking problem.

In the third stage, the drinker is addicted to alcohol. He has no control over his drinking or his behavior and becomes aggressive and apt to fight with his family, friends, or employers. In the final, most severe phase, he suffers the physical and mental deterioration of the chronic alcoholic.

Not everyone who drinks becomes dependent on alcohol; nor do people with serious drinking problems necessarily degenerate into chronic alcoholics. But in a society where alcohol is readily available and the pressures to use it are strong, the potential for abuse is always present.

With the exception of places where Prohibition prevails

Eerie backdrop as lightning flashes in darkened sky over grim scene of a car accident near Worthington, Minnesota, on May 27, 1970, in which one man died and three others were injured. According to the National Safety

under local option, every community in the country has at least one bar or cocktail lounge and a number of liquor stores as well. Few parties are considered complete without beer or whiskey, business meetings are often conducted over cocktails, and drinks are served regularly in many private homes.

Because alcohol is our most socially acceptable drug,

Council, in 1973 there were 55,800 motor vehicle deaths, over half of which were directly attributable to consumption of alcohol.

people tend to forget that it is also our most widely abused drug, ranking far ahead of marijuana as one of this country's major social problems.

Approximately 100 million Americans drink, and approximately one out of every ten is an alcohol abuser. Alcoholism costs the nation $25.3 billion annually in medical expenses, motor vehicle accidents, and lost working days,

"It was like Christmas coming early," said one teen-ager as the Travis Street Electric Co. of Dallas, Texas, poured free beer at midnight on August 27, 1973, to a group of 18-year-olds. It was their first legal drink in the state of Texas. The Dallas night spot was filled to overflowing as some waited, but most didn't, for the date to change from 8/26 to 8/27; with the date change, 18-year-olds became adults in the state.

not to mention the uncounted damage in wrecked lives and broken families.

Alcohol abuse is responsible for at least 50 percent of the nation's automobile fatalities. It is a factor in half of all the homicides and a quarter of all the suicides. It is also involved in 25 percent of the falls, burns, and other accidents that occur in the home, as well as in a large number of hunting, boating, swimming, private flying, and skiing accidents.

While researchers at the National Institute on Alcohol Abuse and Alcoholism are concerned about the nation's ten million problem drinkers, they are particularly alarmed at the sharp rise in drinking among American teenagers. Coupled with this phenomenon there has been an enormous increase in the use of alcohol, particularly by teenage girls and by junior high school students, many of them only twelve and thirteen years old. Most alarming of all, however, is the discovery that one out of twenty young Americans is currently battling a drinking problem and that many more seem destined to join them.

While many aspects of alcohol and alcoholism remain a mystery, there is no question that it is a powerful drug. Like all powerful drugs, it must be viewed with respect and used with restraint. Alcohol can be delightful, but it can also be a poison, a source of pleasure or a serious problem. Only common sense, moderation, and a clear understanding of what alcohol is, and does, can make the difference.

Bibliography

ASBURY, HERBERT, *The Great Illusion, an Informal History of Prohibition*, Doubleday & Co., Inc., Garden City, N.Y., 1950.

BRASCH, R., *How Did It Begin?*, David McKay Co., Inc., New York, 1965.

EMERSON, EDWARD RANDOLPH, *Beverages, Past and Present*, G. P. Putnam's Sons, New York, 1908.

FORBES, PATRICK, *Champagne, the Wine, the Land, the People*, Reynal & Co. in association with William Morrow & Co., New York, 1967.

FURNAS, J. C., *The Life and Times of the Late Demon Rum*, G. P. Putnam's Sons, New York, 1965.

HACKWOOD, FREDERICK W., *Inns, Ales and Drinking Customs of Old England*, Sturgiss & Walton Co., New York, 1909.

LICHINE, ALEXIS, *Encyclopedia of Wines & Spirits*, Alfred Knopf, New York, 1967.

LOLLI, GIORGIO, M.D., *Social Drinking, the Effects of Alcohol*, Collier Books, New York, 1961.

MOREWOOD, SAMUEL, *Inebriating Liquors*, W. Curry, Jun. and Company, and W. Carson, Dublin, 1838.

ROUECHÉ, BERTON, *The Neutral Spirit*, Little, Brown, Boston, 1960.

SINCLAIR, ANDREW, *Prohibition: The Era of Excess*, An Atlantic Monthly Press Book, Little, Brown, Boston, 1962.

SMITH, W. H., AND HELWIG, F. C., *Liquor, the Servant of Man*, Little, Brown, Boston, 1939.

About the Book

Alcohol has been intriguing and intoxicating people for at least seven thousand years. This fascinating history of alcohol begins with the caveman, who probably drank mead made from fermented honey, and ends with the shocking statistics about the recent rapid increase in teen-age alcoholism.

According to the Bible, wine was discovered by Noah, who planted the first vineyard when he left the ark. But an ancient Persian legend credits King Jamshid with the discovery of wine, and it was he who named it "the delightful poison." Champagne was discovered by a 17th-century Benedictine monk named Dom Pérignon, who, when he tasted it for the first time, is supposed to have remarked, "I am drinking stars." These and many other anecdotes fill this lively and exciting book. There are also fascinating chapters on drinking customs and ceremonies, both ancient and modern; drinking in history, particularly as it affected the outcome of wars; the era of Prohibition; the myths and mistakes made about alcohol down through the ages—as well as the scientific facts about the effects of drinking—all described in a clear and colorful way.

About the Author

Alice Fleming is the author of some fifteen books, including *The Senator from Maine: Margaret Chase Smith; Reporters at War; Pioneers in Print;* and *Psychiatry: What's It All About?* She and her husband both write full time. They live surrounded by books, typewriters, and four grown children in a New York apartment and spend their summers in an old house in Westbrook, Connecticut.

Index

Adams, Samuel, 52
akvavit, 13
al kuhul, 11, 12
alcohol: as abused drug, 127–31; blood levels of, 123–25; denatured, 85; as depressant, 121, 123; discovery of, 3–14; and disease, 116–19; ethyl, 3, 121; as medicine, 111–14, 117; metabolism of, 121–23, 125; methyl, 85
alcohol poisoning, 123–24
Alcoholics Anonymous, 110
alcoholism, 107–9, 119–20, 126–27, 131; treatment for, 109–10
ales (celebrations), 29
Allemanni tribe, 6
American Federation of Labor, 91
American Temperance Union, 66
Antabuse, 109
Anti-Saloon League, 75–78
aqua vitae, 12, 112
Arthur, T. S., 69
Association Against Prohibition, 90

Babcock, Orville E., 55
Bacchus, 26–28
bathtub gin, 86
Beecher, Lyman, 63–66, 71
beer, 4–6, 10, 24, 55–56, 106, 111, 124
Benedictine, 21–22
bitters, 61, 112
Black, James, 72
blackouts, 127
Blaine, James G., 55
blood-alcohol levels, 123–25

Boe, Francis de le, 12
bootleggers, 34, 84–86
Booze, E. C., 37
bourbon, 14, 52–53
Bradford, William, 23
brandy, 12
Brunschwig, Hieronymus, 112
Burchard, Dr. Samuel, 55
burlock, 85

Cannon, James, Jr., 92
Capone, Al, 89
Catholic Total Abstinence Society, 68
Chablis, 21
champagne, 8–10, 32, 106, 125
Charlemagne, 19
chartreuse, 21
chicha, 3
Clark, Dr. Billy J., 63
Cleveland, Grover, 55
cocktails, 36–37
Coffey, Aeneas, 13–14
cognac, 12
Cold Water Army, 72–74
Commandaria, 17–18
Connecticut Society for the Reformation of Morals, 65
Constitutional Liberty League, 90–91
Cook, Capt. James, 3, 22
corks, 9–10
Craig, Elijah, 52
Crusaders, 90
customs, drinking, 24–32
Cyaxares, 16

delirium tremens, 118–19
denatured alcohol, 85
dependence: physical, 127; psychological, 126, 127

135

Diamond, "Legs," 89
digestion, of alcohol, 121–23, 125
Dionysus, 24–26
disease, and alcohol, 116–19
distillation, 11–12
Domesday Book, 19
Donovan, Dennis J., 88
Dow, Neal, 71, 72
Drambuie, 18
"Drinker's Dictionary, The" (Franklin), 37–42
drinking: ceremonies and customs, 24–32; English laws on, 100–6; language of, 33–43; myths and misconceptions, 116–20
drunkard's coat, 101
drunkenness, 37–43, 59, 99–107, 119, 123–24
D.T.'s, 118–19
Dutch courage, 33–34

Edward the Elder, 19
Eighteenth Amendment, 75, 77–95
Einstein, Izzy, 88–89
ethyl alcohol, 3, 121

fermentation, 3
Fifteen Gallon Law, 71
Flanagan, Betsy, 36
Francis I, King of France, 21
Franklin, Benjamin, 37–42

Gamay grape, 19
Geber, 10–11, 12
Genghis Khan, 100
genièvre, 13
gin, 12–13, 14
Gin Act (1736), 104

Gin Fever, 103–6
Grant, Ulysses S., 54–55
Greeks, 15–16, 18, 24–27, 99, 111, 113

Hamilton, Alexander, 53, 54, 65
Hancock, John, 52
hangovers, 125–26
Hannibal, 16
Harding, Warren G., 78
hatchetation, 76
Hawkins, John H. W., 67
Hayes, Lucy, 74
hek, 6
Henry de Blois, Bishop, 28
Herodotus, 15–16
highball, 37
Hobbes, Thomas, 104
Hobson, Richmond P., 77
Hogarth, William, 103
Holofernes, 15
home brew, 86
Hoover, Herbert, 92, 93, 94
Hull, Isaac, 51
Huss, Dr. Magnus, 108

ibn-Hayyan, Jabir, 10–11, 12
intoxication, 123–24

jakitis, 86
Jamshid, King of Persia, 6–8
Jefferson, Thomas, 56, 65, 106
Jesus Christ, 28
Johnson, Dr. Samuel, 11
Judith, 15
junever, 13

kava, 3
Keeley, Dr. Leslie, 119

Kieft, Willem, 47
Kramer, John F., 82

language, of drinking, 33–43
Liebig, Justus von, 108
Lincoln, Abraham, 54
Livingstone, Dr. David, 3
Louis XVI, King of France, 52
loving cup, 30

McCoy, Capt. Bill, 85
MacDonald, Flora, 18
MacKinnon family, 18
Madison, James, 56
Margaret, Saint, 30
Martin, Saint, 21
Mathew, Theobald, 68
mead, 4, 10
methyl alcohol, 85
Moderation League, 90
Molasses Act (1733), 49
moonshine, 34, 86
Muhammad, 100

Nation, Carry, 75–76
National Prohibition Act. See
    Volstead Act
near beer, 84
Nicander, 113
Noah, 6, 28

Oglethorpe, James, 50
Old Log Cabin, 37
organized crime, 89–90
Osler, Sir William, 113
oxidation, 121–23, 125

Parker, Capt. John, 52
Passover, 28

patent medicines, 117
Paul, Saint, 111
Penn, William, 55
Pérignon, Dom Pierre, 8–10
Philip the Bold, 19
Prohibition: national, 75, 77–
    95; in states, 71, 75
Prohibition Bureau, 82, 86–89
proof, 124–25
Pure Food and Drug Act
    (1906), 117

Revere, Paul, 51
Richard the Lionhearted, 17
Roman Punch, 74–75
Romans, 24, 26–27, 99, 111,
    119
Roosevelt, Franklin D., 93
rum, 22–23, 48–51, 107
Rum Row, 85
rumrunners, 84–85
Rush, Dr. Benjamin, 62–63,
    65, 107, 116
Russell, Howard Hyde, 75
rye, 14, 52–53

St. Valentine's Day Massacre
    (1929), 89–90
Scotch whisky, 13–14
Selim II, Turkish sultan, 17
Seneca, 99
Sheppard, Morris, 78, 92
Skid Row, 35–36
Smith, Alfred E., 92
Smith, Matthew Hale, 67
Smith, Moe, 88–89
sparkling burgundy, 125
speakeasies, 83
Stuart, Prince Charles Edward,
    18
Sunday, Billy, 81
Sylvius, Franciscus, 12
Syrah grapes, 17

tastevin, 32
Taylor, Zachary, 68
temperance movement, 61–80, 107, 116–17. *See also* Prohibition
Ten Nights in a Bar-Room and What I Saw There (play), 69, 71, 116
toasts, 30–31
Todd, Eli, 107–8
Triangular Trade, 49, 52
Turner, J. Edward, 108
Twenty-first Amendment, 94

Union Temperance Society, 63
Usher, Andrew, 14
usquebaugh, 13

Vassar, Matthew, 56
Vendôme, Duke of, 9
Vikings, 6, 32
Villeneuve, Arnauld de, 11–12, 112
vodka, 13
Volstead, Andrew J., 80
Volstead Act (1919), 80, 82, 86, 92, 94

Washington, George, 51, 52, 53–54, 56, 106

Washington Temperance Society, 66–68
Washingtonian Home for the Fallen, 108
wassail bowl, 29
Webb-Kenyon Law (1913), 77
whiskey, 13–14, 34–35, 52–53, 124–25
Whiskey Rebellion (1794), 53–54, 65
Whiskey Ring (1876), 55
white lightning, 34
Willard, Frances, E., 74
Winchester Dole, 28–29
wine, 6–8, 10, 19–21, 28, 31–32, 106, 107, 124
Women's Christian Temperance Union (WCTU), 74, 76, 117
Women's Crusade, 72, 74
Women's Organization for National Prohibition Reform, 92
wood alcohol, 85

yeast, 3

zeher-e-koosh, 8
Zochitl, 37